Financial Reform and Economic Development in China

ADVANCES IN CHINESE ECONOMIC STUDIES

Series Editor: Yanrui Wu, *Senior Lecturer in Economics, University of Western Australia, Australia*

The Chinese economy has been transformed dramatically in recent years. With its rapid economic growth and accession to the World Trade Organisation, China is emerging as an economic superpower. China's development experience provides valuable lessons to many countries in transition.

Advances in Chinese Economic Studies aims, as a series, to publish the best work on the Chinese economy by economists and other researchers throughout the world. It is intended to serve a wide readership including academics, students, business economists and other practitioners.

Titles in the series include:

The Evolution of the Stock Market in China's Transitional Economy
Chien-Hsun Chen and Hui-Tzu Shih

Financial Reform and Economic Development in China
James Laurenceson and Joseph C.H. Chai

Financial Reform and Economic Development in China

by

James Laurenceson

Lecturer in Economics, University of Queensland, Australia

Joseph C.H. Chai

Associate Professor of Economics, University of Queensland, Australia

ADVANCES IN CHINESE ECONOMIC STUDIES

Edward Elgar
Cheltenham, UK • Northampton, MA, USA

Published by
Edward Elgar Publishing Limited
Glensanda House
Montpellier Parade
Cheltenham
Glos GL50 1UA
UK

Edward Elgar Publishing, Inc.
136 West Street
Suite 202
Northampton
Massachusetts 01060
USA

A catalogue record for this book
is available from the British Library

Library of Congress Cataloguing in Publication Data
Laurenceson, James, 1973-
    Financial reform and economic development in China / by James Laurenceson,
Joseph C.H. Chai.
        p. cm. – (Advances in Chinese economic studies series)
    Includes bibliographical references.
    1. Finance–China. 2. Monetary policy–China. 3. Banks and banking–China. 4.
Financial institutions–China. 5. China–Economic conditions–2000- I. Chai, C. H.
II. Title. III. Series.

HG187 .C6 L28 2003
332'.0951–dc21

                                                                    2002037930

ISBN 1 84064 988 7

Typeset by Manton Typesetters, Louth, Lincolnshire, UK.
Printed and bound in Great Britain by MPG Books Ltd, Bodmin, Cornwall.

Contents

Figures

Tables

Abbreviations

ADL	Autoregressive distributive lag
AIC	Akaike Information Criterion
BIS	Bank for International Settlements
CAC	Credit allocation control
CBL	Commercial Banking Law (1995)
CITIC	China International Trust and Investment Corporation
DEN	Density of financial institutions
DFL	Domestic financial liberalization
DL	Domestic loan
ECM	Error correction model
EFL	External financial liberalization
EMH	Efficient Market Hypothesis
FD	Financial depth
FDI	Foreign direct investment
FI	Foreign investment
FIC	Financial intermediation control
FRI	Financial repression index
GDP	Gross Domestic Product
GDPCAP	GDP per capita
GITIC	Guangdong International Trust and Investment Corporation
IB	Insider, bank-based (model)
IBCR	Interim Banking Control Regulations (1986)
IMF	International Monetary Fund
MC	Market capitalization ratio
NBFI	Non-bank financial institutions
NDR	Nominal deposit rate of interest
NLR	Nominal loan rate
OS	Outsider, stock market based (model)
PBC	People's Bank of China
PPP	Purchasing power parity
RCC	Rural Credit Cooperative
RIR	Real interest rate
SAFE	State Administration of Foreign Exchange
SBA	State budget appropriation

SBC	Schwarz-Bayesian Criterion
SEZ	Special economic zone
SOB	State-owned bank
SOE	State-owned enterprise
SOIE	State-owned industrial enterprise
SPFE	Shadow price of foreign exchange
SRF	Self-raised funds
TIC	Trust and Investment Company
TPP	Total price performance
TR	Turnover ratio
UCC	Urban Credit Cooperative
VOL	Volatility
WTO	World Trade Organization

Acknowledgements

This book is based on a thesis submitted and accepted for the degree of Doctor of Philosophy at the University of Queensland, Australia. I would foremost like to thank my co-author and supervisor, Associate Professor J.C.H. Chai, from whose comments and suggestions this book has benefited greatly. I would also like to acknowledge the help received from Dr Jon Stanford and Dr Tim Purcell at certain stages during the research. The academic stimulation and friendship provided by Dr Ryan McAllister and Dr Darrian Collins was a godsend.

I am also grateful for the facilities and financial assistance provided by Shimonoseki City University, Japan, where I spent over a year lecturing while this manuscript was being prepared, and to Ms Zhang Yi who assisted me greatly during numerous research trips to China.

The publishers wish to thank the following who have kindly given permission for the use of copyright material.

Giordano Dell'Amore Foundation for article: 'Financial Liberalization and Financial Depth in China', with Laurenceson, J. and J.C.H. Chai, *Savings and Development*, XXII, 1998, pp. 393–412.
Taylor and Francis Group (http://www.tandf.co.uk) for article: 'The Economic Performance of China's State-owned Industrial Enterprises', with Laurenceson, J. and J.C.H. Chai, *Journal of Contemporary China*, 9, 2000, pp. 21–39.
John Wiley & Sons Ltd for article: 'State Banks and Economic Development in China', with Laurenceson, J. and J.C.H. Chai, *Journal of International Development*, 13, 2001, pp. 211–225.

Every effort has been made to trace all the copyright holders but if any have been inadvertently overlooked the publishers will be pleased to make the necessary arrangements at the first opportunity.

I dedicate this book to my wife Kathy.

JL

1. Introduction

The idea that the functioning of financial systems affects economic development has a long history in the economics literature, dating back at least to Schumpeter (1912). Following Schumpeter, numerous important contributions to this theme were made, most notably the work of Gurley and Shaw (1955) who provided a theoretical basis for a relationship between the functioning of a financial sector and economic development, and Goldsmith (1969) who was the first to empirically confirm the existence of such a relationship using international panel data. In a review of the more recent empirical literature, Levine (1997, pp. 689, 690) concluded that '…broad cross-country comparisons, individual country analyses, and firm-level investigations point in the same direction: the functioning of financial systems is vitally linked to economic growth'. Levine also set out a theoretical framework that illustrates the factors driving the formation of financial intermediaries and markets, and their impact on economic growth (Figure 1.1). The costs of acquiring information and making transactions create an incentive for the formation of financial intermediaries and markets. In ameliorating these costs, financial systems serve several functions including mobilizing savings, allocating resources and exerting corporate control. In performing these functions, the financial sector can contribute to capital accumulation and technological innovation, thus impacting upon the rate of economic growth.

Given that the financial sector provides such basic services necessary for sustainable economic growth, many economists have argued that financial reform has a particularly important role to play in economies undergoing the transition to a market economy (Griffith-Jones, 1995; World Bank, 1996; Hermes and Lensink, 2000). Mobilizing savings for investment, exerting effective corporate governance over reforming state-owned enterprises (SOEs) and selecting non-state firms to finance are all important elements of a successful transition. Financial reform in transitional economies is also more comprehensive than in most developing countries because it involves not only liberalization, but also shaping the structure and functions of the financial system (Long and Sagari, 1991, p. 431). While the functions of financial systems outlined in Figure 1.1 are provided as a matter of course in most market economies, this has not been the case in transitional economies.

Source: Levine, 1997, p. 690.

Figure 1.1   A theoretical approach to finance and growth

Historically, banks in such countries have been largely administrative units, passively facilitating the physical plans of the central government.

Given the apparent importance of financial reform in determining the economic performance of a developing, transitional economy such as China, it is surprising then that the role of finance has been downplayed in the literature examining China's rapid economic growth during the reform period (1978–present). With only a few exceptions (see, for example, Chai, 1981; Byrd, 1983; Tam, 1986), the study of China's financial sector was assigned a distinctly second-fiddle role to other engines of growth such as trade and foreign investment during the 1980s. Even as recently as the mid-1990s, Fry (1995, p. 53), in a review article on the state of the literature concerning financial development and reform in Asia, concluded that, 'Another major hole is the absence of any material on financial reform in China; this fascinating subject warrants a review article in its own right'. While several important works have emerged in recent years on the topic of financial reform (see, for example, Li, 1994; Tam, 1995; Lardy, 1998a), the balance has yet to be fully redressed. Furthermore, the link between financial reform and economic development continues to be poorly understood.

Perhaps the major reason finance has been so downplayed is because the standard view holds that China's financial sector, in contrast to most other areas of the economy, remains, 'essentially unreformed' (Cheng et al., 1997, p. 204). In particular, the central government continues to exercise considerable control over the financial sector. This control can be seen primarily through two stylized facts. First, the activities of state-owned banks (SOBs) have changed little in that most of their lending continues to be directed towards the state sector (see Table 2.1). Second, the interest rates that SOBs levy on loans and offer on deposits are still controlled by the central government connected central bank, the People's Bank of China (PBC). Largely on the basis of these stylized facts, several recent influential works have argued that the apparent lack of financial reform in China represents a drain on an otherwise successful program of economic reform. Li (1994, p. 3), for example, argues that, 'China has kept a low interest rate ceiling for many years, and it has detrimental impacts. Typically, it encourages inefficient investment and distorts financial efficiency'. This view is supported by Lardy (1998a, p. 127) who states, 'Setting lending rates at below market clearing levels ensures excess demand for loans. Political allocation of credit funds, including corruption inevitably results'. Declining rates of profitability in SOBs and SOEs are typically presented as evidence of the inefficiency of China's financial system.

The theoretical foundation of the standard view regarding the effects of China's apparent lack of financial reform is the well known McKinnon–Shaw hypothesis (McKinnon, 1973; Shaw, 1973). These authors contended that com-

mon government interventions in the financial sector, such as repressing interest rates at below market determined levels and directing credit, are fundamental
stumbling blocks to economic growth in many developing countries. It was
argued that interest rate repression has two primary negative effects. First, it
reduces the incentive of economic agents to hold surplus in the form of financial
assets. Thus, the quantity of financial savings forthcoming will be restricted
with negative implications for the rate of investment and economic growth.
Second, if interest rates are fixed at below market determined levels, there will
be an excess demand for credit and the need for an administrative rationing
process is created. As a result, McKinnon–Shaw proponents argue that low
return investments may gain funding at the expense of high return investments.
The policy implication of the McKinnon–Shaw model then, which has been
advocated by several authors in the case of China (Li, 1994, p. 3; Lardy, 1998a,
p. 127), is financial liberalization whereby the market prices and allocates
financial resources.

There are, however, several deficiencies in the above standard view regarding the extent and impact of financial reform in China. As a result, any policy
implications that flow from much of the existing literature could be misleading. First, the theoretical foundation of the standard view regarding the impact
of the current state of financial reform in China is the subject of much debate
in the wider literature. While the McKinnon–Shaw hypothesis was the dominant paradigm during the 1970s, it came increasingly under attack as numerous
countries had disappointing, or even perverse, experiences with financial
liberalization (Diaz-Alejandro, 1985). Fry (1997a, p. 758) states that the
primary reason many experiments with financial liberalization failed was due
to the perverse reaction to higher interest rates by insolvent and/or non-profit
motivated firms. By definition, an insolvent firm is unable to repay its existing loans and hence is not deterred by a higher borrowing cost. It simply
continues, if it can, to borrow whatever it needs to finance its losses. Such
firms bid up the interest rate until normally solvent, profit-motivated firms
cannot access credit or become insolvent due to the high cost of borrowing.
This observation is particularly instructive in the case of China where the
chief borrowers, the SOEs, are often insolvent and/or non-profit motivated.
Even McKinnon himself (McKinnon, 1993), along with other long-time proponents of financial liberalization such as Fry (1997a), have more recently
argued that international country experience has shown that there are prerequisite conditions that must first be met before successful financial liberalization
can be conducted. Fry (1997a, p. 759) summarizes these as follows:

a.   Adequate prudential regulation and supervision of financial institutions
      and markets.
b.   A reasonable degree of price stability.

c.   Fiscal discipline taking the form of a sustainable government borrowing requirement that avoids inflationary expansion of reserve money by the central bank.
d.   Profit maximizing, competitive behavior by financial institutions.
e.   A tax system that does not impose discriminatory taxes on financial intermediation.

As many countries, including China, have yet to satisfy the above prerequisite conditions, a growing body of literature has emerged which argues that well designed government intervention can be preferable to a fully liberalized financial system in terms of promoting economic development (Stiglitz, 1994; Hellman et al., 1997). Therefore, government intervention in China's financial sector cannot be dismissed as being damaging to economic development a priori.

Second, the dominant methodology presented in the existing literature, which uses financial criteria such as profitability to evaluate the economic performance of China's SOBs and SOEs, is inadequate. The use of financial criteria to evaluate the internal efficiency of a firm or bank can be misleading because these variables can move in opposite directions. Whereas internal efficiency reflects the quantity of output attainable from a quantity of inputs, financial performance reflects revenues relative to costs. The declining financial performance of SOBs also need not reflect allocative inefficiency in their lending. This is because it has long been recognized that projects that have great development significance may only yield a marginal financial return, if at all (Kane, 1983, p. 16). That is, due to the existence of market failures, there is often a large divergence between social and private returns to lending. For this reason, Stiglitz (1994, p. 23) argues that there can be no presumption on the basis of economic theory that a liberalized financial sector will optimally allocate credit. The exclusive use of financial measures to gauge the performance of SOEs and SOBs is also inappropriate in that they are trying to satisfy a range of objectives (economic development objectives, social objectives, and so on) in contrast to firms and banks in a purely market economy that are solely attempting to maximize profits.

Third, the standard view regarding the extent of financial reform in China and its impact on economic development appears to be incongruent with several basic observed facts. For example, the fact that since 1978 China has experienced one of the fastest rates of economic development in modern history has been widely established (Chai, 2000). This is extremely difficult to reconcile with the standard view that China's financial system grossly distorts the optimal allocation of loanable funds. The standard view implies that China would have grown even faster without government intervention in the financial system, which is possible, but not very probable. Another example is the fact that China has experienced rapid financial deepening during the reform period. This is extremely difficult to reconcile with the standard view that the financial sector remains unreformed and that the returns on financial assets have been seriously repressed at low levels by the government. If interest rates had been seriously repressed, surplus agents would have held little incentive to hold financial assets and hence financial depth should have remained low. The declining market share of SOBs and the vast institutional diversification that has taken place is also difficult to reconcile with the view that the financial sector has experienced little real reform. Largely as a result of this institutional diversification, it has been reported that 51 percent of new loans extended by China's financial system in the first half of 2001 went to non-state-owned enterprises (*Asia Times*, 26 September 2001).

In light of the fact that the standard evaluation of financial reform in China lacks a robust theoretical foundation, often uses a questionable methodology and appears at odds with basic observed facts, the objectives of this book are twofold. First, it aims to further the understanding of the nature and extent of financial reform in China. Second, it will examine the impact of financial reform on economic development in China during the reform period. This will enable a more accurate assessment of the Chinese approach to financial reform to be made, and therefore allow more informed policy choices to be made in the future for both China and other developing and transitional economies.

To tackle these issues, the book is divided into eight chapters. Following this introductory chapter, Chapter 2 examines the nature and extent of domestic financial liberalization (DFL) in China. It begins with a review of the reforms that have taken place in the three areas where the government has historically intervened in the financial sector, namely, interest rate controls, credit allocation controls and financial intermediation controls. Following this, a financial repression index is constructed to shed light on the overall trend in DFL and to determine whether in fact meaningful reform has taken place. The second part of Chapter 2 investigates the relationship between DFL and financial depth in China, which is currently an area of confusion in the existing literature.

Chapters 3 and 4 are devoted to investigating the efficiency of SOEs and SOBs. Chapter 3 considers this issue from the perspective of the SOEs. It first presents a theoretical framework that illustrates why financial performance measures such as profitability are deficient as measures of economic efficiency. An empirical exercise is then conducted which directly estimates the change in SOE total factor productivity over the period 1978–97. The chapter then concludes by discussing the various factors, apart from declining internal efficiency, which have contributed to low levels of SOE profitability.

Chapter 4 considers the issue from the perspective of the SOBs. It begins with a discussion concerning the behavior and objectives of the SOBs. This is necessary to determine the appropriate criteria by which to evaluate their performance. Following this, the impact of SOB lending on economic development is directly considered using econometric techniques. Various conceptual reasons why SOBs lending to SOEs should not automatically be taken as evidence of allocative inefficiency are then presented.

While the existing literature has devoted considerable attention to the study of SOEs, and to a lesser extent the SOBs, Chapter 5 examines China's non-bank financial institutions (NBFIs). It begins by chronicling their development during the reform period. Following this, the ownership, control and industrial structure of NBFIs is discussed. The impact NBFIs can have on economic development is then briefly reviewed from a theoretical perspective before the situation in China is evaluated using available data.

While the preceding chapters mainly focus on credit markets, Chapter 6 discusses China's rapidly developing stock markets. Although several studies have been completed on China's stock markets from a financial economics perspective, there have been few, if any, systematic attempts to gauge their impact on economic development. Chapter 6 begins with a review of the nature and extent of stock market development in China. The theoretical and empirical literature examining the relationship between stock markets and economic development is then briefly reviewed before the situation in China is evaluated using available data.

Chapters 2–6 primarily focus on issues pertaining to domestic financial sector reform in China. Chapter 7 switches the focus to the external financial liberalization (EFL) that has taken place during the reform period. This is a much under-studied aspect of China's reform program. The discussion begins by reviewing the nature and extent of EFL that has taken place. An interesting outcome of this discussion is that it is shown that China has not been a large net capital importer, despite economic theory suggesting that it should have been on the basis of its low capital–labor ratio. An empirical analysis is then conducted to establish whether this finding can be at least partly explained by the slow pace of EFL. The chapter then discusses from a theoretical perspective whether China can look upon EFL as a means to promote greater levels of economic development in its current state.

Chapter 8 first provides a summary of the key findings of the study. It then highlights the policy implications of the analysis for other developing, transitional economies, and for China's future financial reforms.

2. Domestic financial liberalization and financial depth in China

INTRODUCTION

As noted in the introductory chapter, the existing literature examining financial reform in China displays several shortcomings. At the most basic level, the trend in DFL has yet to be clearly established. On one hand, the SOBs continue to allocate most of their loans to the state sector of the Chinese economy (Table 2.1). On the other hand, the SOBs have experienced a declining market share (Table 2.2) as a result of vast institutional diversification (Table 2.3). The rapid financial deepening that has taken place during the reform period is also indicative of substantial financial reform (Table 2.4). Therefore, the initial aim of this chapter is to shed light on the complex issue of whether in fact meaningful DFL has taken place.

DOMESTIC FINANCIAL LIBERALIZATION IN CHINA

This section begins by tracing reforms in the three areas where the government has traditionally intervened in China's financial sector; interest rate controls, financial intermediation controls and credit allocation controls. An account of the recent institutional reform of the PBC is also provided. An overall financial repression index for the reform period is then constructed which captures changes in the above policy variables.

Interest Rate Controls

The pre-reform period has been described as the 'dark ages for interest rates' (Yi, 1994, p. 77). During this time interest rates were fixed at negligible levels and rarely varied. In general, DFL should ultimately be revealed indirectly through rising real interest rates. Once interest rate ceilings are removed and financial institutions begin competing for loanable funds, there will be an upward pressure on the deposit rate of interest. Lending rates will also then be free to accurately reflect risk. It has, therefore, become common for researchers to analyse interest rate trends as a guide to determining whether

Table 2.1   The direction of state-owned bank loans

	SOB loans to the state sector (% of total SOB loans)
1978	91.1
1979	90.5
1980	89.5
1981	89.1
1982	89.1
1983	89.1
1984	86.1
1985	87.5
1986	86.9
1987	86.3
1988	86.1
1989	87.7
1990	87.7
1991	88.0
1992	87.9
1993	88.2
1994	91.5
1995	92.3
1996	92.4
1997	94.6
1998	94.5
1999	94.6

Note: Loans to the non-state sector are taken to be those directed to urban and township collective enterprises, domestic private and individual proprietors and the agricultural sector.

Sources:
1.   ACFB, various years.
2.   PBC, 2000, p. 89.

in fact DFL has taken place. Table 2.5 shows the often presented movements in real deposit and loan interest rates in China during the reform period.

According to these figures, the real interest rate has become negative on several occasions when inflation escalated. A rising trend is certainly not observable. For some this serves as evidence that no meaningful DFL has taken place in China's financial sector. This conclusion, however, should be viewed with caution for several reasons. With respect to deposit rates, in September 1988 the Chinese authorities implemented the Long Term RMB

Table 2.2   The market share of state-owned banks

	Deposits held by SOBs (% of deposits held in all financial institutions)	Loans extended by SOBs (% of loans extended by all financial institutions)
1978	87.2	97.6
1979	86.1	97.7
1980	86.1	97.7
1981	86.4	96.7
1982	85.9	96.3
1983	85.1	95.6
1984	85.2	93.1
1985	85.5	93.7
1986	82.7	90.4
1987	80.3	87.6
1988	78.4	86.1
1989	78.9	86.2
1990	83.1	85.8
1991	82.2	84.6
1992	80.5	82.1
1993	78.4	80.3
1994	72.5	79.5
1995	72.2	77.9
1996	72.3	77.6
1997	72.8	79.2
1998	72.9	79.1
1999	73.5	78.6

Note: Aggregate deposit and loan data for all financial institutions in China is available only since 1990. Prior to this time, the total is estimated by adding the figures for SOBs, Rural Credit Cooperatives (RCCs), Urban Credit Cooperatives (UCCs) and Trust and Investment Companies (TICs). Aggregate UCC and TIC data is available only since 1986.

Sources:
1.   ACFB various years.
2.   PBC, 2000, pp. 89, 90.

Value Protected Savings Deposit Plan (World Bank, 1990, p. 54). Under this plan, long-term savings deposits (maturity period of three years or greater) in the state banking system became inflation-proofed through the linking of the nominal return to changes in the overall retail price index. This policy en-sured that the real return on long-term deposits remained strongly positive

Table 2.3 *The institutional structure of China's financial system (year end 1999)*

Name of Institution	Year established	Ownership	Assets
1. Central Bank			
People's Bank of China (PBC)	1948	State	
2. State Commercial Banks			
Agricultural Bank of China (ABC)	1979	State	22 758
Industrial and Commercial Bank of China (ICBC)	1984	State	35 399
Bank of China (BOC)	1979	State	26 181
Construction Bank of China (CBC)	1979	State	22 011
3. Policy banks			
State Development Bank of China	1994	State	688
Export and Import Bank of China	1994	State	59
Agricultural Development Bank of China	1994	State	794
4. Small and medium banking institutions			
Regional commercial banks (10)	1980s	Various	1 450
City commercial banks (90)	1990s	Joint-stock	555
Prefectural level urban credit cooperatives (836)	1990s	Collective	120
5. Foreign banks	1980s	Private/ joint venture	32
6. Non-bank financial institutions			
County level urban credit cooperatives (approx. 2 500)	1980s	Collective	n/a
Rural credit cooperatives (41 755)	1950s	Collective	1 430
Trust and investment companies (239)	1980s	Various	632
Finance companies (69)	1980s	Various	216
Leasing companies (15)	1980s	Various	18
Insurance companies (28)	1980s	Various	–
Postal savings network	1986	State	–

Notes:
1. All asset values are in units of RMB billion with the exception of foreign banks, which are in $US billion.
2. In this study, 'n/a' indicates that data was unavailable.
3   'Various' means ownership consists of state, joint-stock and private ventures.

Sources:
1. Pei, 1998, p. 323.
2. PBC, various years.
3. *ACFB* various years.
4. PBC, 2001, p. 56.
5. Scher, 2001, p. 18.

Table 2.4   Financial depth in China

Year	Financial depth
1978	0.19
1979	0.26
1980	0.29
1981	0.33
1982	0.35
1983	0.37
1984	0.39
1985	0.43
1986	0.50
1987	0.54
1988	0.50
1989	0.54
1990	0.65
1991	0.71
1992	0.75
1993	0.84
1994	0.85
1995	0.90
1996	0.99
1997	1.09
1998	1.18
1999	1.30
2000	1.34

Note: Financial depth is measured as broad money minus currency in circulation, divided by nominal GDP.

Sources:
1. International Monetary Fund (IMF), *International Financial Statistics Yearbook* (*IFS*), various years.
2. *ACFB* various years.
3. PBC, 2001, pp. 96, 97.

even during periods of high inflation (McKinnon, 1994, p. 453). For example, when inflation averaged 18.2 percent over 1988 and 1989, the effective return on long-term savings deposits was increased to over 20 percent (Table 2.6). A similar outcome took place when inflation rose during 1993–95 (*ACFB 1995*, CE, p. 513; *1996*, p. 468).

Table 2.5   Real interest rates in China, 1978–2000 (%)

	NDR	NLR	ORPI	RDR	RLR
1978	3.24	5.04	0.7	2.52	4.31
1979	3.78	5.04	2.0	1.75	2.98
1980	5.04	5.04	6.0	−0.91	−0.91
1981	5.40	5.04	2.4	2.93	2.58
1982	5.67	7.20	1.9	3.70	5.20
1983	5.76	7.20	1.5	4.20	5.62
1984	5.76	7.20	2.8	2.88	4.28
1985	6.72	7.74	8.8	−1.91	−0.97
1986	7.20	7.92	6.0	1.13	1.81
1987	7.20	7.92	7.3	−0.09	−0.81
1988	7.68	8.28	18.5	−9.13	−8.62
1989	11.12	11.15	17.8	−5.67	−5.65
1990	10.02	10.16	2.1	7.76	7.89
1991	7.92	8.88	2.9	4.88	5.81
1992	7.56	8.64	5.4	2.05	3.07
1993	9.41	9.87	13.2	−3.35	−2.94
1994	10.98	10.98	21.7	−8.81	−8.81
1995	10.98	11.52	14.8	−3.33	−2.86
1996	9.21	11.04	6.1	2.93	4.66
1997	7.17	9.84	0.80	6.32	8.97
1998	5.03	7.56	−2.6	7.83	10.43
1999	3.40	6.26	−1.4	4.87	7.77
2000	2.25	5.85	0.4	1.84	5.43

Note: The nominal deposit rate of interest (NDR) is measured by the official one year time savings deposit rate for urban and rural households. The nominal loan rate (NLR) is measured by the official one year working capital loan rate for SOEe. When the nominal interest rate changed during a year, a weighted average has been constructed. The real interest rate (RDR, RLR) is calculated as (1 + Nominal Interest Rate) / (1 + Expected Inflation) − 1. Expected inflation is proxied by current inflation, which is measured by the overall retail price index (ORPI).

Source: ACFB various years.

Therefore, while the deposit interest rates offered by the SOBs continue to be regulated by the government, the administered rate has ensured that the incentive to hold savings deposits has been retained. It should also be noted that the institutional diversification that has taken place in the financial sector during the reform period has led to considerable flexibility with respect to setting deposit rates. For example, in the late 1980s, NBFIs such as Rural

Table 2.6   Effective return on three-year time savings deposits, 1988–89 (%)

	Nominal rate	Cost of living adjustment	Effective return
1988:IV	9.72	7.28	17.00
1989:I	13.14	12.71	25.85
1989:II	13.14	14.59	25.73
1989:III	13.14	13.64	26.78
1989:IV	13.14	8.36	25.50

Source: ACFB 1990, CE, p. 187

Credit Cooperatives (RCCs) were allowed to charge deposit rates up to 70 percent higher than the official rate. Urban Credit Cooperatives (UCCs) and Trust and Investment Companies (TICs) were given a 20 percent upward margin (World Bank, 1990, pp. 25, 146; Yang, 1996, p. 30). Therefore, in comparison with many other developing countries, China's ability to maintain positive real deposit rates has been widely acknowledged (World Bank, 1993a, p. 206; Mehran et al., 1996, p. 68).

With respect to lending rates, it should be remembered that the figures presented in Table 2.5 are the official lending rates used by SOBs when extending loans to SOEs. This is effectively a minimum interest rate for loans. The actual nominal rate charged can vary from this minimum depending on the recipient of the loan and the financial institution extending it. The PBC first allowed some flexibility for SOBs in 1983 when floating interest rates were introduced for certain types of working capital loans (World Bank, 1988, p. 264). Floating rates meant that financial institutions could autonomously set interest rates within a specified band around the official rate. The degree of interest rate flexibility afforded to financial institutions has primarily been tied to macroeconomic conditions; that is, there has been less flexibility during inflationary episodes. Currently, interest rate flexibility is greatest with respect to loans made to non-state-owned enterprises and smaller scale firms (*ACFB 1999*, p. 22). NBFIs also enjoy more flexibility than SOBs (*ACFB 2000*, p. 27). At times, RCCs have been able to charge interest rates on working capital loans up to 90 percent higher than the official rate (World Bank, 1990, p. 25). The extra flexibility afforded to NBFIs has often represented an avenue through which SOBs could avoid the interest rate controls imposed on them. This is because, until financial reforms in 1994, many NBFIs were attached to SOBs (Yi, 1994, p. 255). It became common practice for SOBs to channel business through an associated NBFI in order to avoid more rigid controls over their own operations (Dipchand et al., 1994, p. 110).

The establishment of a relatively free interbank market in 1986 also represented an important means by which SOBs could lend to NBFIs and earn higher rates of return on loanable funds (World Bank, 1990, p. 30; Kumar et al., 1997, pp. 11, 12).

Direct capital raising markets have also become increasingly popular during the reform period with rates of return in these markets being considerably higher than that offered by most financial intermediaries. Since 1984, a number of local enterprises have been able to issue shares and corporate bonds. While a more complete discussion of the stock market in China will be provided in Chapter 6, it will suffice to say here that the rate of return on enterprise shares rose as high as 20–40 percent during 1985–86 and 50–100 percent in 1988 (Mehran et al., 1996, pp. 30, 31). The return on corporate bonds can be up to 40 percent higher than the yield on savings deposits with corresponding terms (*ACFB 1997*, EE, p. 185).

Finally, rising disposable incomes and continued regulation of formal financial institutions have also provided the incentive for the development of unregulated informal financial markets. Feder et al. (1989, p. 511) estimated that up to two-thirds of all rural credit in China is extended through informal channels. Tam (1991, p. 517) cites sample survey evidence showing that interest rates in informal markets have generally been in excess of 20 percent per annum. In addition, while most SOB loans are allocated to SOEs in the first instance at the minimum interest rate, this may not be the final rate at which credit funds are intermediated. Instead of using allocated funds directly for their own investment, there have been numerous reports of SOEs on-lending at higher interest rates for profit (World Bank, 1988, p. 323, 1990, p. 30; Yang, 1996, p. 154). It has been reported that the interest rate for such lending reached between 20–25 percent in 1989 (World Bank, 1990, p. 31).

Financial Intermediation Controls

In many developing countries financial institutions are often required to hold reserves with the central bank that are well in excess of that which could be justified on prudential grounds. This is generally a quasi fiscal measure on the part of government aimed at collecting seigniorage revenue. While it may be effective for this purpose, the degree to which financial institutions can effectively perform an intermediary role is adversely affected. Excessively high reserve requirements can mean that potentially productive financial resources are left idle.

Formal reserve requirements in China were first introduced in 1984, coinciding with the introduction of a two-tiered banking system in which the PBC was instituted as the central bank (Chai, 1998, pp. 122, 129). In 1985, the reserve requirement for SOBs was set at 10 percent. However, for much of their history, reserve requirements have been nearly double this level. Throughout most of the 1990s, the reserve requirement was set at 13 percent and in addition, SOBs were required to hold excess reserves of around 5–7 percent (Mehran et al., 1996, p. 44). This high reserve ratio policy was reversed in 1998 when the formal required reserve ratio was reduced to 8 percent and then again to 6 percent in 1999. It is unlikely, however, that the initial rise in the reserve requirement increased the level of financial repression by reducing the overall level of intermediation provided by the SOBs. This is because, for a variety of reasons (Girardin, 1997, p. 59), China's SOBs have generally held reserves that have been in excess of that required. Similarly, when the reserve requirement was reduced by 5 percent in 1998, the resultant liquidity was frozen in order to purchase treasury bonds. Only the liquidity created by the 2 percent reduction in 1999 was at the SOBs' disposal (*ACFB 2000*, p. 19).

Direct intermediation controls such as credit ceilings specified in the annual credit plan have been of far greater consequence. This traditional tool of credit control set limits on the total lending of each financial institution and sub-ceilings for certain categories of loans (World Bank, 1990, p. 37). The credit plan meant that even if financial institutions were able to collect more deposits, their ability to increase lending was restricted. The extent to which the details of the credit plan have actually been enforced has varied considerably during the reform period. For example, after strictly enforcing credit quotas in 1985 in response to accelerating inflation, credit ceilings effectively became indicative targets in 1986 and excess lending was not penalized (World Bank, 1988, p. 298). In this period there also began a trend towards allowing financial institutions to extend additional loans if more deposits could be collected (Chai, 1998, p. 124). However, when inflation again accelerated in the late-1980s and the mid-1990s, credit ceilings were more strictly enforced. Nevertheless, during the 1990s the overall trend has been away from direct controls and by 1995 only the major SOBs remained subject to any credit ceilings (Mehran et al., 1996, pp. 42, 50). In 1998, credit ceilings for the SOBs were also abandoned in favor of asset–liability management principles (PBC 1998, p. 14). It should be noted that the government still influences the volume of SOB lending through an annual guiding plan. This plan sets recommended targets for incremental lending based on macroeconomic conditions and is designed to be used as a reference document upon which SOBs should formulate their own plans. Evidence from the most recent years suggests that the guiding plan has in fact been used quite aggressively by the PBC to influence credit volume and structure and that the SOBs have followed it closely. For example, when economic growth began slowing in 1998, the PBC stated that SOBs were able to temporarily depart from asset–liability management principles such as the loan–deposit ratio in order to meet the targets specified in the guiding plan. Furthermore, the SOBs could apply for additional PBC relending if their own funds were insufficient (*ACFB 1999*, pp. 15, 19).

Credit Allocation Controls

The allocation of credit in China has also traditionally been determined through the credit plan. It specified in a detailed manner the sources and use of funds by economic sectors and types of enterprises (Chai, 1981, p. 41). As with the credit ceilings contained in the plan, the extent to which the allocative details have been enforced has varied considerably during the reform period. During the mid-1980s the details became merely indicative and sectoral credit allocation was largely discontinued. Local bank branches were given greater latitude with respect to loan approvals instead of merely applying directives issued by their headquarters. Projects approved by the state plan no longer obtained automatic credits and banks retained a right of refusal (Chai, 1998, pp. 124, 130). Financial reforms in 1994 saw the formation of three policy banks whose purpose it was to allow the rest of the SOBs to concentrate on more commercially oriented lending. A new Commercial Banking Law (CBL) issued in 1995 also emphasized the need for financial institutions to incorporate commercial criteria into their lending practices (*ACFB 1996*, pp. 182–199, 244–260). Despite the official demise of the credit plan in 1998, as with the overall volume of credit, the government continues to influence the credit structure through the annual guiding plan issued to SOBs (*ACFB 1999*, p. 19).

Determining the precise level of credit directed by the government in China is not possible due to a lack of data and a universally accepted definition as to what actually constitutes directed credit. However, applying two simplifying assumptions to the available data can yield a useful indicator of the degree of government involvement in credit allocation. First, it can be assumed that all the credit extended by SOBs to the state sector is directed. In the context of China's official statistics regarding SOBs, this involves subtracting from the total, loans made to the agricultural sector, township and village enterprises, private enterprises and individual proprietors. Ideally, some component of loans made to foreign-funded enterprises would also be subtracted, however, a complete data series is not available and hence this item is retained for the sake of maintaining comparability with earlier years. Second, it can be assumed that the lending of all other financial institutions (that is, other banks and NBFIs) is not directed. Generally speaking, these institutions have been far more independent in their operations and have come outside the plans of the central government and PBC (Yi, 1994, p. 255). Of course not all SOBs loans to the state sector are in fact policy directed.

Some SOEs no doubt would be able to attract credit even in a fully liberalized financial system. Similarly, not all loans extended by other financial institutions have been free from government interference. For example, varying degrees of government interference in the lending of TICs and RCCs have been well established and will be discussed further in Chapter 5. These components, however, cannot be separated from the available statistics. The intensity of government involvement in the allocation decisions of China's financial sector can then be taken to be SOB loans to the state sector, divided by the total lending of all financial institutions. This data is presented in Table

Table 2.7   Government involvement in the credit allocation decisions of China's financial sector

	%
1978	88.89
1979	88.42
1980	86.55
1981	86.22
1982	85.86
1983	85.23
1984	80.14
1985	81.95
1986	78.54
1987	75.64
1988	74.10
1989	75.25
1990	75.21
1991	74.44
1992	72.18
1993	70.85
1994	72.76
1995	71.97
1996	71.65
1997	74.88
1998	74.77
1999	74.41

Note: See note 1, Table 2.2.

Sources:
1.   Laurenceson and Chai, 1998, p. 402
2.   *ACFB*, various years.

2.7 and indicates a gradual trend of decline in directed credit since 1978. The adequacy of this proxy measure of directed credit is also reassuring as it accurately captures known periods where the government temporarily increased control over financial institutions in response to internal macroeconomic disturbances such as inflation in 1985, 1989 and 1994, and external disturbances such as the Asian financial crisis in 1997.

Institutional Reform of the People's Bank of China

Whereas the significant impact of institutional diversification on financial liberalization can largely be discussed in terms of a reduction in interest rate controls and credit allocation controls, one of the most important aspects of financial reform in recent years has been the institutional reform of the PBC. Until 1998, the branch network of the PBC was based on the Chinese administrative system, with 31 branch offices located at the provincial level. The problem with this system is that it provided government officials at the provincial level with significant leverage to influence the decision making of the PBC's branch offices. This situation often had negative implications for the allocative efficiency of capital as provinces duplicated investments and pet projects of local administrators were able to attract funding. As a result, the PBC underwent three phases of reform in 1998. During the first phase (May–August), the PBC simplified its supervisory role by transferring the responsibility for supervising securities and insurance business to the China Securities Regulatory Commission and the China Insurance Regulatory Commission respectively. During the second phase (September), 148 city-level PBC branches that were deemed to be duplicating tasks were either closed or merged. Finally, during the third phase (November–December), the 31 provincial branches of the PBC were replaced by 9 regional branches that were in a better position to conduct unified monetary policy and financial supervision (PBC 1999, p. 53).

The Overall Trend in Financial Liberalization in China

In order to gain an overall picture of the trend in DFL, the approach adopted by Demetriades and Luintel (1996a and 1996b, 1997) for other developing countries such as India and Nepal is used in this research. Based on a series of underlying policy variables describing the extent of financial repression (such as interest rate controls, reserve requirements, directed credit and so on), these authors constructed a summary index of financial repression using the statistical method of principal components. In the context of this research, the underlying variables describing financial repression in China have been discussed above; namely, interest rates controls (IRC), financial intermediation controls (FIC) and credit allocation controls (CAC). The ability to construct a single financial repression index (FRI) using principal component analysis relies upon the fact that trends in financially repressive policies tend to move in the same direction. For example, it is rare for a government to loosen interest rate controls while at the same time increasing the proportion of directed credit. Based on this premise, principal component analysis (see Duntamen, 1989, pp. 15–23; Demetriades and Luintel, 1996a, p. 363) can linearly transform a set of positively correlated variables $X_1,\ldots, X_k$ into a new, smaller set of variables $Z_1,\ldots, Z_k$, which are termed principal components. These new variables have two important properties. First, they are not correlated with one another and second, they are ordered in terms of the amount of variance in the original variables they explain. Therefore, the first principal component frequently explains the vast majority of variance in the initial set of $X_1,\ldots, X_k$ variables. Principal components are obtained by using the latent roots and latent vectors of the $X'X$ matrix, where X is the nsk matrix of n observations on $X_1,\ldots, X_k$. Thus,

$$Z = XA \qquad (2.1)$$

where $A = [a_1, a_2,\ldots, a_k]$, $a_1, a_2,\ldots, a_k$ are the latent vectors corresponding to the latent roots $\lambda_1, \lambda_2,\ldots, \lambda_k$ respectively and $\lambda_1 > \lambda_2,\ldots > \lambda_k$. In the empirical literature, latent roots and vectors are frequently termed eigenvalues and eigenvectors respectively. In order to develop a simple FRI in the case of China, data are arranged in Table 2.8 with respect to IRC, FIC and CAC. Trends in CAC are captured by using the indicator of the intensity of directed credit presented in Table 2.7, which is defined as SOB loans allocated to the state sector expressed as a percentage of total financial institution lending. It could also be argued that this measure to some extent captures interest rate liberalization as financial institutions apart from the SOBs were given considerably more flexibility with respect to interest rate determination. Nevertheless, a separate attempt is made to crudely capture changes in IRC by using a dummy variable that is assigned a value of 1 when interventions in the pricing of credit were highly rigid and 0 when controls were relaxed. Therefore, in light of the earlier discussion, it is assigned a value of 1 until 1987. Similarly, a dummy variable is used to crudely describe changes in FIC, where a value of 1 indicates that credit ceilings were strictly enforced while 0 signifies periods when ceilings were indicative in nature or absent entirely. A value of 1 is therefore assigned for 1978–85, 1989–91 and 1994. The eigenvalues and eigenvectors derived from the correlation matrix of financial repression variables are presented in Table 2.9.

Based on these results, the next consideration is how many principal components should be retained for the calculation of a FRI. As discussed by

Table 2.8   An overall financial repression index for China, 1978–99

Year	IRC	FIC	CAC	FRI
1978	1	1	88.89	56.13
1979	1	1	88.42	55.84
1980	1	1	86.55	54.69
1981	1	1	86.22	54.48
1982	1	1	85.86	54.26
1983	1	1	85.23	53.87
1984	1	1	80.14	50.72
1985	1	1	81.95	51.84
1986	1	0	78.54	49.19
1987	1	0	75.64	47.40
1988	0	0	74.10	45.87
1989	0	1	75.25	47.12
1990	0	1	75.21	47.09
1991	0	1	74.44	46.62
1992	0	0	72.18	44.68
1993	0	0	70.85	43.86
1994	0	0	72.76	45.04
1995	0	0	71.97	44.55
1996	0	0	71.65	44.35
1997	0	0	74.88	46.35
1998	0	0	74.77	46.28
1999	0	0	74.41	46.06

Note: FRI is calculated in time period t as $\text{FRI}_t = 0.574\,(\text{IRC}_t) + 0.537\,(\text{FIC}_t) + 0.619\,(\text{CAC}_t)$.

Table 2.9   Eigenvalues and eigenvectors of the correlation matrix of financial repression variables

Variable	Eigenvectors (a_k)		
	a_1	a_2	a_3
IRC	0.574	0.600	0.557
FIC	0.537	0.789	0.298
CAC	0.619	0.128	0.775
Eigenvalues (λ_k)	2.437	0.463	0.100

Duntamen (1989, pp. 22–23), the literature offers only somewhat ad hoc rules of thumb. Some authors have recommended dropping those principal components of a correlation matrix with eigenvalues of less than 1. Others have subsequently argued that such a recommendation was too restrictive, preferring a cut-off of 0.7. Another approach is to retain enough principal components to explain a desired percentage of the variation in the underlying variables. Other considerations to remember are the more principal compo-nents relative to the number of variables that are retained, the less parsimonious the description of the data will be. In addition, smaller principal components are, in general, harder to interpret than larger ones. Fortunately, from the results presented in Table 2.9, the choice to retain only the first principal component is clear and satisfies all the above rules of thumb and other considerations. The first principal component accounts for 2.437/3 = 81.2 percent of the variance in the three underlying variables. Other results (not presented) also show that all of the underlying original variables are highly correlated with the first principal component, with a correlation coefficient of 0.896 for IRC, 0.838 for FIC and 0.966 for CAC. Furthermore, the first principal component has the benefit of being easily interpreted as an overall

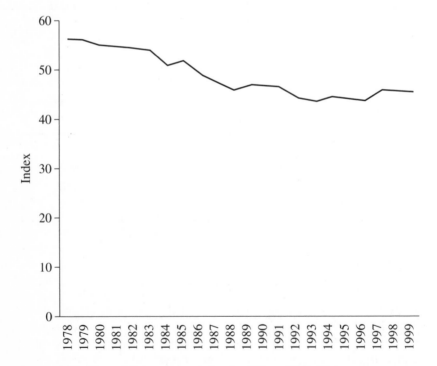

Figure 2.1   Financial repression index for China, 1978–99

measure of financial repression because the calculated eigenvector assigns relatively equal weights to each of the three variables; 0.574 for IRC, 0.537 for FIC and 0.619 for CAC. Finally, it is obviously the most parsimonious choice. An overall FRI can therefore be constructed by linearly transforming the underlying variables according to the eigenvector associated with the first principal component. This FRI is presented numerically in Table 2.8 and plotted in Figure 2.1. The FRI indicates a gradual trend towards DFL during the reform period. While the overall level of DFL in China may be modest compared with other developed, market economies, it has nonetheless increased in terms of a Chinese historical perspective.

THE RELATIONSHIP BETWEEN FINANCIAL LIBERALIZATION AND FINANCIAL DEPTH: THEORETICAL ASPECTS

Given that China has experienced some DFL during the reform period, the observed rapid increases in financial depth may not be so surprising. In this section, the theoretical literature on the effects of DFL on financial depth is first reviewed. According to the standard McKinnon–Shaw theoretical view, DFL will have a positive impact on financial depth and economic growth by restoring the incentive of surplus agents to hold financial assets. The essential features of the McKinnon–Shaw model are presented in Figure 2.2. Savings S_{g_0}, at a rate of economic growth g_0, is a positive function of the real rate of interest r. The demand for those savings to fund investment I, is a negative function of r. Financial repression is illustrated here as an administratively determined nominal interest rate fixed initially at r_0, which holds r below its equilibrium value, r_E. At r_0, surplus agents have little incentive to hold financial assets and as a result, the amount of investment is constrained to I_0. In addition to the quantity of investment, the McKinnon–Shaw theory also contends that interest rates fixed at low levels will reduce the productivity of investment because they cannot perform a screening role. Instead credit must be administratively rationed. If the nominal interest rate increased to r_1, reflecting partial DFL, this would have two beneficial effects. First, financial deepening would occur as the incentive to hold financial assets increases. This then permits the amount of investment that can be undertaken to increase to I_1. Second, low return investments with a yield between r_0 and r_1 would be rationed out. Previously, some of these investments may have received credit during the administrative rationing process. Hence, the average efficiency of investment is assumed to increase. This process increases the rate of economic growth and is shown through a rightward shift in the savings function to S_{g_1}. Thus, the new situation can be depicted by r_1, I_1.

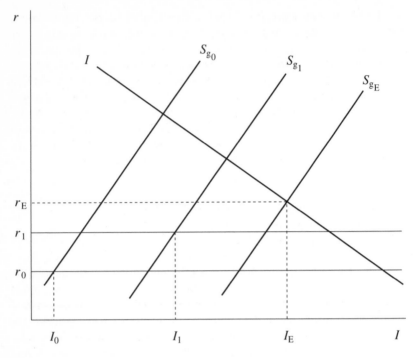

Source: Fry, 1982, pp. 732, 733.

*Figure 2.2   Domestic financial liberalization and financial depth: the
               McKinnon–Shaw model*

According to the McKinnon–Shaw theory, abolishing interest rate ceilings
altogether is the optimal policy approach in order to maximize the amount of
investment and the efficiency of investment. This is shown in Figure 2.2 by
the equilibrium r_E, I_E and a higher rate of economic growth g_E.

While still informative, in recent years several deficiencies in this standard
theoretical model have been raised. First, the role of financial institutions is
strictly passive. Financial institutions are treated as perfect competitors that
transform deposits into loans at zero cost (Demetriades and Luintel, 1996b,
p. 361). As a result, there is little scope to analyse the behavior of financial
institutions and the emphasis is therefore placed on the way in which the
interest rate influences aggregate savings and investment. The assumption
that financial institutions are perfectly competitive is an extreme one, particularly in the context of a developing country such as China. It is also of
concern because earlier research has already pointed out that whether government intervention will lead to more or less financial intermediation is partly

dependent upon the market structure of the banking sector. For example, Courakis (1984) showed that under monopoly banking, a ceiling on the loan interest rate could result in a higher deposit rate of interest and volume of deposits and loans by changing the marginal revenue schedule of the bank. A second limitation of the standard model is that it only allows for the volume of savings to be altered by changes in the interest rate. In reality, empirical evidence suggests that until the real interest rate approaches negative values, the interest rate elasticity of deposits is quite low and the volume of savings forthcoming may be affected by a host of other, more important factors (Hellman et al., 1997, p. 168). Demetriades and Luintel (1996b, pp. 361–364), for example, extend the work of Courakis (1984) by developing a model whereby a monopoly bank subject to interest rate controls can also lead to increased financial depth via financial institutions pursuing non-interest rate activities such as advertising and branch proliferation.

Hellman et al. (1997) offers an alternative paradigm to the McKinnon–Shaw framework to understand the relationship between government intervention and financial depth, which they label financial restraint. This alternative paradigm provides various theoretical channels through which well designed, selective government intervention (as distinct from outright financial repression) may actually increase financial depth over and above that which could be achieved through complete financial liberalization. For example, by regulating interest rate spreads at positive but still below market clearing levels, rents can be created that accrue to financial institutions. That is, the profitability of providing a financial intermediation service can be enhanced. The increased profitability of financial institutions could lead to (a) more confidence on the part of savers in the stability of formal financial institutions and hence a greater willingness to hold financial assets independent of interest rate factors, and (b) increased investment in deposit collection infrastructure which will reduce the transaction costs incurred by savers when accessing the formal financial system. This will again have the effect of increasing financial depth in a manner independent of the interest rate.

Figure 2.3 is adapted from Hellman et al. (1997, p. 167) and sets forth a simple demand and supply model of the market for loans that can be used to illustrate the differences between the McKinnon–Shaw framework and the financial restraint approach. In this model of the financial system there are three sectors; the household sector, which supplies savings (S), firms, which demand the savings for investment (I) and financial institutions, which provide a financial intermediation service. In the absence of government intervention, the equilibrium interest rate is r_E and the quantity of funds intermediated is I_E. No rents accrue to financial institutions. Assume now that the government sets the deposit rate of interest at r_D and the loan rate of interest at r_L. Under the McKinnon–Shaw framework this reduces the extent

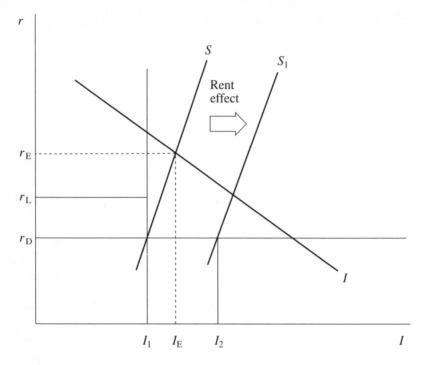

Figure 2.3   A model of financial restraint

of financial intermediation because at the regulated deposit rate of interest, savers are only prepared to supply I_1. However, under the financial restraint viewpoint this standard analysis is deficient because it ignores the effects of rents created as a result of government intervention. After government intervention, the difference between $r_D - r_L$ represents a rent accruing to financial institutions. As noted above, such rents can have the effect of increasing the supply of savings, independent of the level of interest rates. Thus, the simplest manner in which the gains associated with the rent accruing to financial institutions can be depicted is by a rightward shift in the supply curve from S to S_1. If the rent effect is large relative to the interest rate elasticity of savings, then the total volume of funds intermediated will be larger than in the liberalized case ($I_2 > I_E$). It should be noted that the rents created as a result of government intervention might give rise to socially wasteful activities such as corruption resulting from highly profitable banking licenses and do not solve the weaknesses of an administrative credit rationing process. Nevertheless, in terms of theory and beginning from a point of financial restraint, the impact of DFL on the level of financial depth is ambiguous.

FINANCIAL LIBERALIZATION AND FINANCIAL DEPTH: EMPIRICAL EVIDENCE FROM CHINA

The methodology used to examine the empirical relationship between DFL and financial depth (FD) in this research follows that of Demetriades and Luintel (1996a, 1996b, 1997). FD is generally deemed to be a positive function of real GDP per capita (GDPCAP), the real interest rate (RIR) and the density of financial institutions (DEN). The inclusion of GDPCAP draws on the literature on finance and development, which suggests that a symbiotic relationship exists between the development of the financial system and the real economy (Demetriades and Luintel, 1996a, p. 359). In the McKinnon–Shaw framework, the basis for this relationship is the complementarity between money and capital. In the endogenous growth literature, the relationship between financial development and economic growth is based on the ability of financial intermediaries to correct for market failure due to informational problems (Greenwood and Jovanovic, 1990) or production externalities (Bencivenga and Smith, 1991). RIR is a theoretically important determinant of FD because the higher the real interest rate, the more incentive economic agents will have to hold surplus in the form of financial assets. As a result, economies with high rates of inflation are often characterized by low levels of financial depth as agents hold alterative stores of value. It is through the inclusion of RIR as an independent variable that most previous studies have indirectly examined the effects of financial repression on FD and economic growth (Gelb, 1989). The rationale for including DEN is straightforward; the greater the access economic agents have to financial institutions and markets, the lower the transaction costs are of holding financial assets.

In light of the earlier theoretical discussion, the most obvious shortfall in this standard specification is that it fails to consider the possibility that financial repression may directly impact on financial depth via avenues apart from RIR. To address these issues, the approach suggested by Demetriades and Luintel (1996a and 1996b, 1997) is followed whereby the earlier calculated FRI is included as an additional explanatory variable. This approach is useful because it allows for financially repressive policies to directly impact on financial depth in the econometric modeling procedure while at the same time not causing an excessive loss of degrees of freedom. The expected sign of FRI cannot be determined on a-priori theoretical grounds.

The data sources and notes on the construction of each variable are as follows. The time period covered by the data is 1978–99. The total number of observations is restricted to 21 due to the existence of only annual observations for some variables. FD is taken from Table 2.4. In this table, FD is measured as broad money minus currency in circulation, divided by nominal GDP. Without deducting currency in circulation, the measure is primarily one of monetization, not financial depth (Demetriades and Luintel, 1996a, p. 360). RIR is measured by the real one-year savings time deposit rate presented in Table 2.5. To measure DEN, the number of persons employed in the financial sector per 10,000 of population is used. Employment statistics are used because data on the number of financial institution branches are incomplete. The source is SSB (various years). The data for GDPCAP are also calculated from this source. All data are presented in the Appendix (Table A1).

To model financial depth, an autoregressive distributive lag (ADL) modeling approach to cointegration of the type pioneered by Pesaran and Pesaran (1997) and Pesaran and Shin (1999) is used. This approach features numerous advantages over more traditional methods. For one, the econometric methodological benchmark of the General-to-Specific approach pioneered by Davidson et al. (1978) begins with a fairly unrestricted dynamic model and imposes restrictions in order to capture the data generating process. An ADL model that has a sufficient number of lags to capture the data generating process is an example of such a General-to-Specific modeling framework. Second, from an ADL model, a dynamic error correction model (ECM) can be derived through a simple linear transformation (Banerjee et al., 1993, p. 51). The ECM addresses the issue of integrating short-run dynamics with the long-run equilibrium without losing long-run information. The third advantage of using the ADL approach is that it avoids problems resulting from non-stationary time series data. The dangers of estimating an econometric model using non-stationary data are well known (Charemza and Deadman, 1997). The Augmented Dickey–Fuller was used to test the stationarity properties of the data in Table A1 and, as expected, the null hypothesis of non-stationarity could not be rejected. Fortunately, Pesaran and Shin (1999) show that the ADL approach can be used to reliably test hypotheses on coefficients when the variables are integrated of order 0 or 1. They also show that the ADL approach typically outperforms alternative approaches to cointegration such as Phillip and Hansen's Fully Modified Ordinary Least Squares when the sample size is small. Finally, they show that the ADL approach is robust against simultaneous equation bias and autocorrelation so long as the orders of the ADL model are adequately selected on the basis of a-priori knowledge or estimated using a model selection procedure such as the Akaike Information Criterion (AIC) or Schwarz–Bayesian Criterion (SBC).

The ADL approach specifies a maximum lag length to search over the parameter space and model selection is carried out using the SBC. The SBC is used in preference to the AIC because the SBC is more parsimonious with the lag length selection and is a consistent model selection criterion (Pesaran and Shin, 1999). As is recommended by Pesaran and Pesaran (1997, p. 304) the model is estimated using data covering 1978–98, with the final datum in 1999 being saved to test the predictive performance of the model. A maximum number of 2 lags was chosen on the basis that the data are annual in nature and in light of the limited number of observations. The ADL procedure is computationally expensive, needing to evaluate $(p + 1)^k = (2 + 1)^5 = 243$ different equations in order to obtain the optimal lag length. The ADL (2, 2, 1, 1, 0) model was selected by the SBC. The short- and long-run coefficients are presented in Table 2.10, while the associated ECM is presented in Table 2.11.

The overall goodness of fit of the estimated equation is extremely high exhibiting an R^2 of 0.999. This is a feature of ADL models and is due to the presence of lagged endogenous regressors. In addition, the F statistic measuring the joint significance of all regressors is statistically significant at the 1 percent level. The model also passes diagnostic tests for functional form, normality and heteroskedasticity. There is, however, an indication that autocorrelation exists. The issue of autocorrelation in the ADL model is a problematic one. On the one hand, autocorrelation results in unbiased but inefficient estimators, and the consequent weakening of significance tests.

Table 2.10   ADL (2, 2, 1, 1, 0) model results, dependent variable: FD

Coefficient	Regression estimates		Long-run estimates	
	$\hat{\beta}_i$	$S_{\hat{\beta}_i}$ (p-value)	$\hat{\beta}_i$	$S_{\hat{\beta}_i}$ (p-value)
α_0	−0.091	0.299 (0.769)	−0.100	0.325 (0.767)
FD_{t-1}	0.819	0.188 (0.002)		
FD_{t-2}	−0.725	0.142 (0.001)		
$GDPCAP_t$	0.321×10^{-3}	0.264×10^{-3} (0.259)	0.577×10^{-4}	0.916×10^{-4} (0.546)
$GDPCAP_{t-1}$	0.001	0.492×10^{-3} (0.046)		
$GDPCAP_{t-2}$	−0.001	0.325×10^{-3} (0.002)		
RIR_t	0.010	0.001 (0.000)	0.008	0.002 (0.010)
RIR_{t-1}	−0.003	0.001 (0.048)		
FRI_t	0.006	0.003 (0.060)	0.159×10^{-4}	0.005 (0.998)
FRI_{t-1}	−0.006	0.004 (0.160)		
DEN_t	0.026	0.006 (0.003)	0.029	0.007 (0.002)

$R^2 = 0.999$
$F_{(10, 8)} = 991.167$ (0.000)

Diagnostic Tests –
Serial Correlation: $F_{(1, 7)} = 22.783$ (0.002)
Functional Form: $F_{(1, 7)} = 0.012$ (0.914)
Normality: $\chi^2 (2) = 1.138$ (0.566)
Heteroskedasticity $= F_{(1, 17)} = 1.041$ (0.322)

Table 2.11   ADL (2, 2, 1, 1, 0) model ECM results, dependent variable: ΔFD

| Coefficient | Regression estimates | |
	$\hat{\beta}_i$	$S_{\hat{\beta}_i}$ (p-value)
$\Delta\alpha$	−0.091	0.299 (0.767)
$\Delta FD1$	0.725	0.142 (0.000)
$\Delta GDPCAP$	0.321×10^{-3}	0.264×10^{-3} (0.250)
$\Delta GDPCAP1$	0.001	0.325×10^{-3} (0.001)
ΔRIR	0.010	0.001 (0.000)
ΔFRI	0.006	0.003 (0.051)
ΔDEN	0.026	0.006 (0.001)
ECM_{t-1}	−0.906	0.177 (0.000)
$R^2 = 0.958$		

Note: Notation is as follows: $\Delta\alpha = \alpha_t - \alpha_{t-1}$; $\Delta FD1 = FD_{t-1} - FD_{t-2}$; and so on.

Those variables that are significant will still remain so in the presence of autocorrelation. The question is whether variables that are non-significant are in fact non-significant due to autocorrelation. However, it should be noted that, as mentioned above, the ADL approach has been shown to be robust against residual autocorrelation. The presence of autocorrelation in the estimated ADL model is due to the lagged endogenous regressors and would disappear with a reduction in lag length. However, the order of the model has been selected on the basis of the SBC and thus a reduction in lag length would result in a non-optimal model specification. In summary, the presence of autocorrelation does not affect the parameter estimates and the model selected is optimal based on the SBC.

Two general features of the ECM associated with the ADL (2, 2, 1, 1, 0) model are particularly worth noting. First, the error correction term is highly statistically significant. This significance points to a long-run cointegrating relationship between the variables. It should also be recalled that the long-run coefficients presented in Table 2.10 form the long-run equilibrium in the error correction term. Second, the coefficient to the error correction term is extremely high at −0.906, which suggests a rapid speed of adjustment back to long-run equilibrium following a short-run shock. Specifically, it states that more than 90 percent of the disequilibria in a previous year is corrected for in the current year. This econometric finding is consistent with observations of financial depth in China. For example, when inflation rose sharply in 1989 and 1994, rapid financial disintermediation took place. However, as soon as real interest rates were increased and anti-inflationary measures put in place, savers once again began quickly building up their holdings of savings deposits.

With respect to individual variables, the signs of the estimated long-run coefficients in all cases conform to a-priori expectations. The results indicate that RIR and DEN have had the most pronounced impact on financial depth in both the long and short run. RIR in the current period and the estimated long-run coefficient are both positive and significant at the 1 percent level. The ECM also shows that ΔRIR, the change in RIR, is a significant determinant of ΔFD, the change in FD, at the 1 percent level. The estimated coefficients to DEN are the largest in quantitative terms amongst the included explanatory variables and are significant at the 1 percent level in both the short and long run. In the ECM, ΔDEN, the change in DEN, is significant in explaining ΔFD at the 1 percent level. The estimated long-run coefficient to FRI is extremely small and statistically insignificant. However, ΔFRI, the change in FRI, narrowly misses statistical significance in explaining ΔFD at the 5 percent level. Thus, FRI appears to exhibit a greater impact in the short run. Despite the strengths of the estimated model, it should be noted that its predictive performance for the year 1999 was poor. This outcome is most likely due to the limited number of available observations. Data problems in the case of China mean that the results of any econometric analyses need to be interpreted with caution and remain subject to revision as more data become available.

CONCLUSION

This chapter has shown that in contrast to many standard assertions, China has experienced gradual DFL since 1978. It was also shown that while the government has been, and continues to be, involved in determining the interest rates offered by the SOBs, a positive return on savings deposits has largely been maintained. While the extent of DFL may appear limited relative to other, more developed market economies, it should nonetheless be viewed in the appropriate context, that being a Chinese historical perspective. The finding that China has undergone some DFL is informative because otherwise the observed rapid increases in financial depth are difficult to explain. The econometric investigation conducted suggests that the key facets of financial reform that have led to increased financial depth are the maintenance of positive, real deposit interest rates and the institutional diversification that has contributed to increasing financial institution density.

3. The performance of China's state-owned industrial enterprises

INTRODUCTION

Given that the SOBs lending to SOEs is a basic stylized fact in China's financial sector, understanding the performance of these groups is fundamental to evaluating the efficiency of the Chinese approach to financial reform. Chapter 3 considers the issue from the perspective of the SOEs. If it can be shown that the internal efficiency of SOEs has improved/worsened, then the implications of SOBs lending to SOEs can be viewed in a more/less favorable light.

For reasons of data availability, the experience of China's state-owned industrial enterprises (SOIEs) is examined as a case study and the time period is restricted to 1980–1997.[1] Industry is a useful focal point for the research because it is the largest sector in the Chinese economy and one in which state-owned units continue to play an important role. In 1997, SOIEs produced 41 percent of gross industrial output value, controlled 64 percent of fixed assets used in industrial production and employed 65 percent of all industrial workers (SSB, 1998, pp. 432, 444, 448). The experience of SOIEs is also illustrative because while they have experienced a substantial decline in their financial performance during the reform period (Table 3.1, column 1), the share of total SOB credit allocated to them has not declined (Table 3.2). Given that declining profitability is often taken to be evidence of worsening internal efficiency, it is such a combination of factors that typically underlies the standard view that China's financial sector grossly distorts the optimal allocation of loanable funds.

However, the hypothesis that the declining financial performance of SOIEs can be attributed to worsening internal efficiency is immediately questionable because industrial firms not owned by the state have also experienced a decline in profitability (Table 3.1, columns 2–5). Therefore, to single out SOIEs as being particularly inefficient without further investigation would be inappropriate. The likelihood of a sector-wide decline in efficiency is extremely doubtful, and in the case of industrial enterprises, such a conclusion is incongruous with the findings of a growing body of research directly measuring their total factor productivity (TFP) (Wu, 1993; Jefferson et al., 1992, 1996, 2000).

Table 3.1 *Profitability of industrial enterprises in China, 1980–97, by ownership type (%)*

	State		Collective		Shareholding		Foreign		HK/Macao/ Taiwan	
	A	B	A	B	A	B	A	B	A	B
1980	37.0	23.9	58.6	40.8						
1981	35.3	22.1	47.2	30.7						
1982	34.6	21.3	43.7	27.5						
1983	34.0	21.1	46.0	29.6						
1984	35.2	21.5	45.7	28.5						
1985	36.2	20.0								
1986	31.5	16.2								
1987	30.9	16.1								
1988	31.5	15.8								
1989	27.1	11.4	32.2	16.1						
1990	19.9	5.1	23.9	8.7						
1991	18.9	4.6	25.1	9.5						
1992	19.0	5.2	29.7	13.5						
1993	20.7	6.9	30.9	13.8	48.2	32.2	32.3	21.5	21.3	13.8
1994	21.0	6.1	29.3	11.0	39.5	23.7	23.1	13.2	19.3	10.1
1995	16.4	3.8	24.2	11.2	29.0	16.0	23.0	12.2	12.5	6.2
1996	12.4	1.9	22.2	8.6	22.7	11.6	19.1	9.7	12.1	5.7
1997	11.9	1.7	21.7	8.4	20.7	10.8	17.4	8.6	11.9	5.8

Notes:
1. Profit is calculated as profit/average net fixed capital stock. Prior to 1993, only year-end figures for net fixed capital stock are available. An arithmetic average of consecutive year-end figures is used in these years.
2. A and B refer to pre-tax and after tax profitability respectively.
3. Data for shareholding, foreign and HK/Macao/Taiwan owned-firms are not available prior to 1993. Data for collective owned-firms during 1985–88 were not available for this study.

Sources:
1. *Zhongguo Gongye Jingji Ziliao 1949–1984*, p. 85.
2. SSB, various years.

Given that the internal efficiency of SOIEs is not immediately clear, the primary objective of this chapter is to shed light on the relationship between financial performance and internal efficiency and consider the empirical data in the case of SOIEs. A theoretical framework is first provided that illustrates the relationship between these two variables. It is shown that financial per-

*Table 3.2   The share of total state-owned bank loans allocated to state-
              owned industrial enterprises*

	%
1978	19.0
1980	17.7
1985	16.7
1990	23.5
1995	22.3
1999	22.8

Source: ACFB, various years.

formance not only reflects changes in TFP, but also changes in the firm's total price performance (TPP), or the change in the price the firm receives for its output relative to the price it must pay for its inputs (that is, terms of trade). Therefore, instead of evaluating the SOIEs' performance using 'catch all' financial criteria, trends in the SOIEs' TFP and TPP are investigated separately. Finally, numerous other reasons are noted that help to explain the low level of SOIE profitability apart from their level of internal efficiency.

THEORETICAL FRAMEWORK

To illustrate the relationship between internal efficiency and financial performance, a theoretical framework outlined by Waters (1997) is useful. Consider a firm operating over two time periods, 0 and 1, where output quantities and prices, and input quantities and prices, are for notational convenience expressed in the form of index numbers. The firm's revenue (R) in each time period can be expressed as

$$R_0 = P_0 \times Y_0 \quad \text{and} \quad R_1 = P_1 \times Y_1 \tag{3.1}$$

and total costs (C) as

$$C_0 = W_0 \times X_0 \quad \text{and} \quad C_1 = W_1 \times X_1 \tag{3.2}$$

where P_0 and P_1 are output prices; Y_0 and Y_1 are output quantities; W_0 and W_1 are input prices; and X_0 and X_1 are input quantities. Profit (π) can be defined as the ratio of revenue to costs

$$\pi_0 = \frac{R_0}{C_0} \quad \text{and} \quad \pi_1 = \frac{R_1}{C_1} \tag{3.3}$$

Following from this, changes in profitability can be expressed as

$$\frac{\pi_1}{\pi_0} = \frac{R_1/C_1}{R_0/C_0} \quad \text{and} \quad \frac{P_1 Y_1/W_1 X_1}{P_0 Y_0/W_0 X_0} \tag{3.4}$$

To illustrate the link between financial performance and internal efficiency, the right-hand side of equation (3.4) can be rearranged as follows

$$\frac{\pi_1}{\pi_0} = \underbrace{\frac{Y_1}{Y_0} \times \frac{1}{X_1/X_0}}_{\{TFP\}} \times \underbrace{\frac{P_1}{P_0} \times \frac{1}{W_1/W_0}}_{\{1/TFP\}} \tag{3.5}$$

That is, changes in firm profitability can be decomposed into two parts. The first is changes in internal efficiency, or TFP. Increasing TFP can assist in improving financial performance because from a given quantity of inputs, the firm can now produce a greater quantity of saleable output. The second determinant is TPP. Accounting for changes in TPP reflects the fact that revenues and costs are determined not only by quantities, but also prices. The link between internal efficiency and financial performance is not tight because constant TPP over time is not the norm.

In the case of China's SOIEs there are at least two reasons why TPP is likely to have declined during the reform period. First, SOIEs have been subject to increased competition from non-state firms (Naughton, 1992). Increased competition in product markets is likely to have put downward pressure on output prices, while increased competition for certain factors of production such as skilled labor is likely to have driven up input prices. Second, TPP is likely to have declined due the changing nature of price determination in China's transitional economy (Chai, 1998, pp. 94–117). Prior to economic reform in 1978, many SOIEs were given priority in the purchase of production inputs at prices fixed at below equilibrium levels. In addition, the price of output in many industrial sectors was fixed at exceptionally high levels. However, as the reform program gained pace, SOIEs increasingly faced market determined prices, or fixed prices that had been revised so as to more accurately reflect relative scarcity. The notion that the financial performance of SOIEs prior to economic reform benefited from limited competition and the administrative pricing system is evidenced by the fact that over the period 1958–78, they were able to achieve an average before tax profit to net fixed asset ratio of 40 percent, despite evidence which suggests that they experienced, at best, only minor improvements in TFP (SSB, 1992, p. 385; Chen et al., 1988).

TOTAL FACTOR PRODUCTIVITY IN CHINA'S STATE-OWNED INDUSTRIAL ENTERPRISES, 1980–97

This section directly considers the internal efficiency of SOIEs by providing annual estimates of TFP growth covering the period 1980–97. Unfortunately, the estimates can only be conducted until 1997 because the data collection process for several necessary variables has changed significantly in recent years. The methodological approach and data sources used broadly follows that of Jefferson et al. (1992, 1996, 2000), which have come to represent a benchmark in the literature examining changes in the SOIEs' TFP during the reform period. Whilst the reliability of the official Chinese statistics used by these authors has come under some criticism (see Woo et al., 1994), they mount a detailed defense in their 1996 paper and find no empirical support for the argument that TFP estimates for SOIEs will be biased or subject to serious measurement error (Jefferson et al., 1996, pp. 156–166). Other prominent researchers have also verified the overall internal consistency of official Chinese statistics (Chow, 1986). Simply put, China's statistical system remains largely an administrative one, rooted in the centrally planned economy (Ren, 1997, p. 23). This has meant that state-owned units tend to be well accounted for. Most inadequacies are confined to non-state-owned units, where the State Statistical Bureau has had to rely on the submissions of local government officials who may have incentives to falsify statistics (Jefferson et al., 1996, p. 163). Since this chapter focuses only on SOIEs, the approach of Jefferson et al. (1992, 1996, 2000) is therefore justificatory. The final data used to calculate TFP are presented in Table 3.3, which is followed by a brief discussion of the data. A more detailed treatment of the derivation and sourcing of each series is given in the Appendix (Tables A2–A5).

To calculate DGV, nominal gross output value is deflated by an ex-factory price index for industrial output. The Urban Survey Team of China's State Statistical Bureau constructs this price index. DNPF is attained in a two-step procedure. First, the proportion of fixed assets owned by SOIEs that are not used to produce industrial output are subtracted from total fixed assets. SOIEs typically own a substantial amount of fixed assets not connected with their industrial activities since they provide employees with a wide range of benefits such as subsidized housing. Second, a fixed investment deflator is applied to annual net investment increments in order to arrive at a constant price measure of net fixed assets. For the period 1980–92 an index constructed by Jefferson et al. (1992, 1996) is used. This is because an official fixed investment deflator only became available in 1991. The Jefferson et al. (1992, 1996) index uses movements in factory construction costs and equipment costs to proxy for price changes in fixed investment. It is interesting to note that there is very little difference between this index and the official index in

Table 3.3   *Productivity data for China's state-owned industrial enterprises,*
              1980–97

Year	DGV	DNPF	DINT	LAB
1980	658.66	493.50	572.85	27.01
1981	674.50	503.45	590.03	28.28
1982	723.73	524.43	634.07	29.37
1983	792.99	548.52	683.89	29.99
1984	873.67	568.45	715.70	30.37
1985	972.32	615.40	740.48	31.48
1986	1 055.34	675.40	740.48	33.02
1987	1 135.01	724.65	822.96	33.85
1988	1 227.99	786.99	841.70	35.13
1989	1 236.00	858.18	816.90	35.57
1990	1 257.05	930.01	824.85	36.07
1991	1 353.27	1 016.04	866.61	37.35
1992	1 506.89	1 107.13	924.34	37.51
1993	1 570.53	1 208.69	825.82	37.88
1994	1 505.40	1 334.18	818.37	37.24
1995	1 340.68	1 535.77	694.13	36.82
1996	1 373.33	1 713.68	705.14	36.44
1997	1 406.22	1 787.24	701.83	34.94

Note:
DGV – Value of gross industrial output;
DNPF – Value of average net fixed assets used in industrial production;
DINT – Value of intermediate inputs;
LAB – average number of employees engaged in industrial production.
The unit for DGV, DNPF and DINT is billion yuan and all are expressed in terms of constant 1990 prices.
The unit for LAB is million workers.

Source: See Appendix (Tables A2–A5).

the common years of 1991 and 1992. This consistency is reassuring and suggests that both are an adequate guide to price movements in newly added fixed assets. The official fixed investment deflator is used after 1992. To estimate DINT, net output value (value added) is subtracted from gross output value along with two other minor accounting items. This nominal series is then deflated by a price index of intermediate inputs used by industrial enterprises. Since 1984, the Urban Survey Team of the China's State Statistical Bureau has constructed such an index and hence is the choice for this research. Prior to 1984, an index constructed by Jefferson et al. (1992) is relied upon that begins in 1980 and extends until 1988. It is worthwhile mentioning that in the common years of 1984–88, the official series increases at a greater rate than the one devised by the above authors. If this situation also holds prior to 1984, and if the reliability of the official index is assumed, the constant price measure of intermediate inputs will be over-estimated leading to TFP estimates being biased downwards. This of course cannot be verified since official data are lacking prior to 1984. LAB is attained by taking away those employees not directly involved in industrial production from the total SOIE labor force.

Using these basic data, trends in partial factor productivity are presented in Table 3.4. The growth rate of output and inputs, along with TFP calculations are presented in Table 3.5. TFP is calculated in each year as

Table 3.4   *Partial factor productivity in China's state-owned industrial enterprises, 1980–97*

	Fixed assets	Intermediate inputs	Labour
1980	1.33	1.15	24 383
1981	1.34	1.14	23 851
1982	1.38	1.14	24 644
1983	1.45	1.16	26 444
1984	1.54	1.22	28 767
1985	1.58	1.31	30 888
1986	1.56	1.36	31 958
1987	1.57	1.38	33 534
1988	1.56	1.46	34 955
1989	1.44	1.51	34 753
1990	1.35	1.52	34 851
1991	1.33	1.56	36 236
1992	1.36	1.63	40 177
1993	1.30	1.90	41 461
1994	1.13	1.84	40 423
1995	0.87	1.93	36 415
1996	0.80	1.95	37 693
1997	0.79	2.00	40 252

Note: Partial factor productivity of fixed assets is calculated as RMB of real output value per RMB of real net fixed assets used in industrial production (DGV/DNPF). For intermediate inputs it is equal to RMB of real output value per RMB of real intermediate input (DGV/ DINT). For labor it is equal to RMB of real output value per employee engaged in industrial production (DGV/LAB).

$$TFP_t = (\ln DGV_t - \ln DGV_{t-1}) - \alpha_k (\ln DNPF_t - \ln DNP_{t-1})$$
$$- \alpha_m (\ln DINT_t - \ln DINT_{t-1}) - \alpha_l (\ln LAB_t - \ln LAB_{t-1}) \quad (3.6)$$

where ln is the natural log, t indicates the time period and α_k, α_m and α_l are the normalized output elasticity's of fixed assets, intermediate inputs and labor. These have earlier been estimated to equal 0.205, 0.675 and 0.12 respectively (Jefferson et al., 1992, p. 251). Thus, TFP is measured as the change in output not accounted for by changes in inputs.

The partial factor productivity measures of labor and intermediate inputs have risen quite steadily over the reform period. The partial productivity of

Table 3.5   Total factor productivity in China's state-owned industrial enterprises, 1980–97

	Output	Fixed capital	Intermediate inputs	Labor	TFP
1981	2.40	0.41	1.99	0.55	0.58
1982	7.04	0.84	4.86	0.45	0.89
1983	9.14	0.92	5.11	0.25	2.86
1984	9.69	0.73	3.07	0.15	5.74
1985	10.70	1.63	2.30	0.43	6.34
1986	8.19	1.90	3.39	0.57	2.33
1987	7.28	1.45	3.74	0.30	1.79
1988	7.87	1.69	1.52	0.45	4.22
1989	0.65	1.78	−2.02	0.15	0.75
1990	1.69	1.65	0.65	0.17	−0.78
1991	7.38	1.81	3.33	0.42	1.81
1992	10.75	1.76	4.35	0.05	4.59
1993	4.14	1.80	−7.61	0.03	9.91
1994	−4.24	2.03	−0.61	−0.20	−5.44
1995	−11.59	2.88	−11.11	−0.14	−3.22
1996	2.41	2.25	1.06	−0.13	−0.78
1997	2.37	0.86	−0.32	−0.50	2.33
Average	4.74	1.65	0.22	0.86	2.02

Notes:
1. Column (2) shows the growth rate of DGV. Column (3) shows the growth rate of DNPF × 0.205. Column (4) shows the growth rate DINT × 0.675. Column (5) shows the growth rate of LAB × 0.12. Column (6) shows the growth rate of TFP and is calculated as TFP = (2) − (3) − (4) − (5).
2. Figures in columns (2)–(5) have been rounded for presentation purposes. Final TFP figures in column (6) have been rounded only after the calculation has been performed.

fixed assets on the other hand increased initially before beginning a gradual decline since the end of the boom period in the late 1980s. Thus, measures of partial productivity do not paint a clear picture of changes in SOIE efficiency. In any case, the researcher should not rely too heavily on such partial measures as their inferiority to TFP estimates are well known. Of primary importance is that the data indicate TFP trended upward at an average annual rate of 2.02 percent and contributed 43 percent (2.02/4.74) to the increase in real output over the period. This compares with 35 percent for fixed assets, 18 percent for intermediate inputs and 5 percent for labor.

The TFP estimates for each year are clearly sensitive to cyclical fluctuations. For example, TFP slowed markedly and even turned negative during the macroeconomic austerity programs of 1989 and 1994 while rising to extremely high levels during the boom period in between. This can be explained by two factors (Jefferson et al., 1996, p. 166). First, and of particular relevance to SOIEs, factor inputs such as labor are somewhat fixed. Facing an economic downturn, SOIEs would rarely lay off staff despite a fall in the demand for their output. Given that TFP is measured as the change in output not accounted for by changes in inputs, fixed factors of production mean that TFP will fall during an economic contraction. Second, TFP estimates will vary with the business cycle because available data do not reflect changes in the capacity utilization of factor inputs. For example, the labor input is measured as the number of employees instead of the number of labor hours actually worked. While SOIEs may not lay off workers during a recession, they are likely to allow them to take extended periods of leave and so the actual number of labor hours worked will decline. The data used in this chapter do not take this decline into account and thus actual TFP will be greater than the estimated figure during contractions and less than the estimated figure during expansions. The trend growth rate of 2.02 percent over the 17-year period, however, should not be affected by this data limitation.

It should also be noted that TFP estimates during more recent years could be underestimated due to the process of SOIE reform. Part of this program has included the transformation of highly productive SOIEs into new ownership forms such as joint venture and shareholding companies (Jefferson et al., 1996, p. 167; Chai and Docwra, 1997, p. 166). This has meant that in subsequent statistical publications these firms have then been classified as non-state-owned enterprises.

TOTAL PRICE PERFORMANCE IN CHINA'S STATE-OWNED INDUSTRIAL ENTERPRISES, 1980–97

Given that TFP has increased since 1980, it can be hypothesized on the basis of equation (3.5) that the decline in financial performance of China's SOIEs is the result of a deterioration in TPP. To test this hypothesis five price indexes are required; one for output and one for each of the three major input categories of fixed assets, intermediate inputs and labor. In addition, an overall input price index can be estimated by weighting the price index of each input by its respective normalized output elasticity.

In calculating TFP in the previous section, price indexes for industrial output, fixed assets and intermediate inputs have already been constructed. A price index of the average unit price of labor in SOIEs is available from the

Table 3.6   Total price performance in China's state-owned industrial enterprises, 1980–97 (1980 = 100)

	P_G	P_K	P_M	P_L	P_I	TPP
1980	100.00	100.00	100.00	100.00	100.00	1.00
1981	100.20	106.05	100.77	99.88	101.75	0.98
1982	100.00	106.53	101.80	101.29	102.71	0.97
1983	99.90	115.25	103.09	102.93	105.56	0.95
1984	101.30	123.48	108.23	125.59	113.44	0.89
1985	110.11	140.91	127.77	145.42	132.58	0.83
1986	114.87	161.25	140.11	169.95	148.02	0.78
1987	123.32	178.92	155.28	187.91	164.04	0.75
1988	141.82	192.48	192.56	226.64	196.63	0.72
1989	168.20	238.00	243.46	255.52	243.79	0.69
1990	175.10	242.12	257.09	282.75	257.10	0.68
1991	185.95	270.93	280.49	308.33	281.87	0.66
1992	198.60	303.86	311.34	351.53	314.63	0.63
1993	246.26	384.73	420.60	428.76	414.23	0.59
1994	294.27	424.68	497.21	546.95	488.31	0.60
1995	338.13	449.86	573.31	656.46	557.98	0.61
1996	347.94	467.78	590.05	720.66	580.66	0.60
1997	346.90	475.73	588.28	755.83	585.31	0.59

Note: Price indexes are for industrial output (P_G), fixed assets (P_K), intermediate inputs (P_M), labor (P_L) and overall inputs (P_I) respectively. TPP is calculated as P_G/P_I.

Source: See text and Appendix Tables A2–A5.

State Statistical Bureau. This price index is a measure of total compensation paid to labor and includes wages, salaries and other payments in kind or cash (SSB, 1999, p. 180). Such additional payments include bonuses, subsidies and allowances extended by SOIEs to employees. It is important that such additional payments are encompassed by the price index because they comprise a sizeable proportion of the total compensation paid to labor. Table 3.6 presents the price index data and the derived TPP.

The data confirm the hypothesis that SOIEs faced a serious decline in TPP with their terms of trade declining by an average of 3.02 percent per year over the period 1980–97. Thus, the decline in profitability of SOIEs is well explained and is indicative of a decline in TPP, not TFP. Figure 3.1 provides a graphical representation of the trends in TFP and TPP since 1980. Both series are presented in index form with 1980 being the base year.

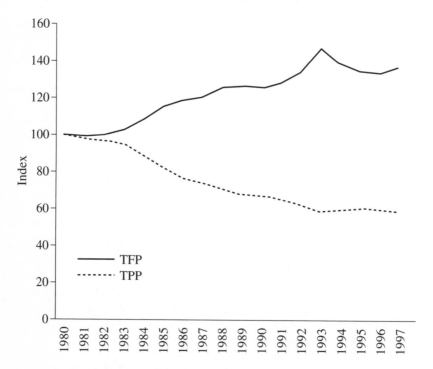

Figure 3.1   Total factor productivity and total price performance in China's state-owned industrial enterprises, 1980–97

OTHER CONSIDERATIONS IN EVALUATING THE FINANCIAL PERFORMANCE OF STATE-OWNED INDUSTRIAL ENTERPRISES

It has been shown that when financial performance is separated into its two components, the internal efficiency of China's SOIEs is considerably more impressive. However, as shown in Table 3.1, the profitability of SOIEs has remained below most of the non-state-owned industrial enterprises. Due to this, it may be argued that the rate of TFP growth in SOIEs was slower than in non-state units. Directly testing this hypothesis is made difficult by data quality concerns but the most recent study by Jefferson et al. (2000) sheds light on the matter. The authors concluded that, during years in which complete data sets were available, the TFP growth performance of SOIEs was less than that of collectively owned firms but was comparable, and in some cases in excess of, other non-state ownership types such as foreign firms and shareholding firms. Therefore, other factors apart from changes in internal efficiency are likely to have led to lower levels of SOIE profitability. One reason could be that SOIEs suffered greater declines in their TPP as compared to firms of other ownership types. The main reason for this assertion is that SOIEs are disproportionately located in areas of industry where output prices have been traditionally set at low levels by the government and have been slow to adjust. Even after two decades of price reform, controls in excavation industries such as energy, fuel and raw materials remain significant (Chai, 1998, pp. 95, 101). Incomplete price reform has meant that firms in these sectors have had perverse terms of trade forced upon them. For example, World Bank (1993b, p. 10) notes that of the 40 industrial sector classifications in China, five earned an abnormally low rate of return on capital. In four of these sectors, this poor financial performance could be directly attributed to the fact that their output prices were fixed at low levels by the government. Expectedly, non-state-owned firms beginning production in the reform period have tended not to locate in these areas of industry (Naughton, 1992, p. 26). Therefore, SOIEs have become obligated to produce such basic outputs. In some habitually loss-making sectors, the SOIE share approaches 100 percent. This compares with just 34 percent in manufacturing and 28 percent in light industry in 1997 (SSB, *CSY 1998*, pp. 444, 448, 453).

Another part of the SOIEs' relatively low after-tax profitability can be attributed to an unequal tax burden (Chai and Docwra, 1997, p. 165). Prior to 1994, SOIEs were subject to a 55 percent income tax rate. At the same time foreign-owned firms paid only 33 percent and those located in special economic zones, 15 percent. It has also been calculated that their indirect tax burden was only 50 percent of that faced by SOIEs. Similarly, collective enterprises enjoyed several tax concessions and their profit tax rate was only 35 percent (Broadman, 1995, p. 45). A further portion of the reportedly lower levels of SOIE profitability can be explained by accounting changes, rigidities in statistical collection procedures and methods of calculating profitability. For example, 77 percent of the profit reduction of SOIEs in 1993 can be traced back to the adoption of new accounting rules in that year (Chai and Docwra, 1997, p. 166). The effect of transforming successful SOIEs into non-state ownership in recent years on the profitability of the remaining SOIEs has already been mentioned. Finally, when profitability is calculated as a percentage of fixed assets (as is typically the case), there is a built-in bias against SOIEs because a significant proportion of their fixed assets are not used to produce industrial output. If this proportion was excluded the profitability of SOIEs would look considerably more impressive.

In evaluating the performance of state-owned units it should also be remembered that their role and objectives are fundamentally different to non-state-owned units in China and in other market economies. For example, SOEs have essentially constituted China's social security system by providing benefits to workers such as retirement pensions, subsidized housing, medical care and child minding facilities (Hu, 1996, pp. 126–129). Obviously the provision of such services will increase costs and so reduce their reported profitability. Bonin and Huang (2001, p. 200) cite evidence that shows between 1980 and 1994, enterprise expenditures on social welfare increased by six times, and that by the mid-1990s, it was equal to roughly half the SOEs' total wage bill. Western economies generally meet such social expenses through the government budget. Hence, part of the lower profitability of SOIEs in China is akin to budgetary expenditure in a Western context.

CONCLUSION

This chapter investigated the internal efficiency performance of SOEs, using SOIEs as a case study. The results showed that in contrast to their declining profitability, SOIEs displayed considerable improvements in internal efficiency. While this result in itself does not confirm the allocative efficiency of the financial system or justify the practice of SOBs lending almost exclusively to SOEs, at the very least it suggests that the development consequences of this stylized fact may not have been as negative as is often assumed. It also prompts further discussion into the specific channels through which the process of financial reform may have contributed to increases in firm productivity. This discussion is undertaken in the following chapter. The finding that SOIEs experienced improvements in internal efficiency despite a declining financial performance is also important because it highlights the potentially misleading nature of much of the existing literature that uses financial criteria to measure changes in efficiency.

NOTE

1. The data used in this chapter is from SOIEs with independent accounting systems. Confining our analysis to SOIEs with independent accounting systems is done for reasons of data availability and does not result in a major loss of coverage with such firms producing 96 percent of total state-owned industrial output in 1997 (SSB, *CSY 1998*, pp. 433, 448).

4. The performance of China's state-owned banks

INTRODUCTION

This chapter considers the economic development implications of the SOBs' lending. Since 1995, China's SOBs have been labeled as commercial banks in official statistical publications and Chinese law. The behavior of a commercial bank in a purely market economy is dictated by its optimization problem, that being, to maximize expected profits subject to a risk constraint (Santeromo, 1984, p. 580). This objective function means that loans, for example, will be allocated to those projects that offer the highest expected rate of financial return. Commercial banks will also diversify their loan portfolios and maintain a strong capital base to more effectively manage risk. Given these objectives, the performance of a commercial bank can largely be determined by examining its balance sheet and calculating measures of financial return such as profitability, and measures of solvency such as capital adequacy.

This has become the standard approach to evaluating the performance of China's SOBs in both academic circles and the mainstream press (Lardy, 1998a, pp. 76–127). The profitability of SOBs has declined markedly since the mid-1980s when they were amongst the most profitable in the world (Girardin, 1997, p. 32). Their pre-tax profit/asset ratio dropped from 1.4 percent in 1985 to just 0.2 percent in 2000 (Lardy, 1998a, pp. 93; *The Banker*, July 2001, p. 164). In a survey of the world's 1000 largest commercial banks taken at year-end 2000, the four largest SOBs, Industrial and Commercial Bank of China (ICBC), Agricultural Bank of China (ABC), Bank of China (BOC) and Construction Bank of China (CBC), achieved a rate of return on assets that ranked 875th, 922nd, 830th and 764th respectively. The comparative soundness of the big four SOBs, as measured by the capital/assets ratio, was also relatively poor despite a RMB270 billion capital injection in 1998, ranking 725th, 541st, 758th, 749th respectively (*The Banker*, July 2001, p. 164). This poor commercial performance has led some commentators to the conclusion that, even in light of the Asian financial crisis of 1997, China possesses the 'The Worst Banking System in Asia' (*The Economist*, 2 May 1998).

There are, however, several deficiencies that can be identified in this standard evaluation of their performance, and in particular with respect to the implications it holds for their role in economic development. First, while China's SOBs may be labeled commercial in name, it would be incorrect to automatically assume that their objectives conform to those of a typical commercial bank found in most Western countries. It is important to remember the historical context from which these SOBs have evolved. Prior to economic transition, their primary objective was to facilitate the implementation of the government's physical plan (Chai, 1998, p. 119). In this context, their performance was simply dependent upon how well they undertook this task. Profitability and risk management were not major concerns. Before any meaningful analysis of their performance during the reform period can be conducted, it is first necessary to consider if their behavior and objectives have changed. Second, as was shown in the previous chapter, financial performance is a poor guide to internal efficiency. It is interesting to note that other financial institutions in China have also experienced a decline in financial performance during the 1990s. For example, the pre-tax profit/assets ratio of non-state-owned commercial banks in China fell from 1.81 percent in 1993 to 0.15 percent in 1996. Profitability of NBFIs such as UCCs also declined from a high of 3.45 percent in 1989 to 0.11 percent in 1996, and in trust and investment companies from 1.75 percent in 1988 to 0.03 percent in 1996 (Kumar et al, 1997, pp. 84, 85, 90; *Zhongguo Jinrong*, various issues). This suggests that other factors, apart from changes in internal efficiency, may have contributed to the decline in the SOBs' financial performance. Standard measures of internal bank efficiency such as the cost/income ratio have actually declined for Chinese banks in recent years from 86.1 percent in 1996 to 64.4 percent in 2000. This current value is on par with banks in large developing countries such as Brazil and those in the transitional economies of Central and Eastern Europe (*The Banker*, July 2001, p. 161). Third, and most important, in the context of assessing the impact of SOBs on economic development, financial performance is a poor guide to the development impact of lending. As was noted in the introductory chapter, due to large divergences between the private and social returns to lending, a project that may be of great development importance could only yield a marginal financial return, if at all. Finally, solely using measures of solvency such as capital adequacy ratios to determine the long-term soundness of SOBs is misleading because they are fully owned and backed by the government.

This chapter begins by examining the behavior of SOBs as a means of determining whether their goals have changed during the reform period. The legal framework surrounding SOBs is then examined in order to further clarify their objectives. In light of this discussion, the performance of SOBs is then evaluated by considering the development impact of their lending, the social impact of their lending and their solvency status.

THE BEHAVIOR OF STATE-OWNED BANKS

To ascertain the suitableness of using commercial measures to gauge the performance of SOBs, it is first necessary to evaluate whether they have begun to pursue commercial objectives during the reform period. If they have, this should be observable through changes in their behavior. The experience of other transitional economies can serve as a useful guide to detecting the emergence of commercial banking behavior. For example, Borish et al. (1997, p. 340) notes that the share of SOB credit allocated towards non-state-owned firms has risen in the case of several central European transitional economies. This is to be expected as old SOBs increasingly take on commercial objectives and diversify their loan portfolios in order to seek profit and better manage risk. The data presented in Table 2.1, however, showed that China's SOBs continue to lend overwhelmingly to the state sector.

If the SOBs have begun to pursue commercial objectives, the direction of their lending should also have become increasingly sensitive to financial returns. The case study of SOIEs already presented in Chapter 3 suggests that the SOBs lending has not become sensitive to financial returns in particular sectors of the economy. For example, Tables 3.1 and 3.2 showed that despite a sharp decline in their profitability, SOIEs continued to attract a constant share of the SOBs' lending. Park and Sehrt (1999) provide a more formal test of whether the behavior of SOBs has become increasingly commercial in nature after the PBC implemented numerous reforms in the mid-1990s, including the relaxation of the credit plan in favor of asset–liability management principles, the recentralization of PBC refinancing to avoid local government interference, the establishment of policy banks and the introduction of a new commercial banking law. The methodology used by Park and Sehrt is based on a model of bank profit maximization, from which econometric tests are derived that examine whether SOBs have become less influenced by government policy objectives and more influenced by financial criteria in lending. Provincial-level data are used over the period 1991–97, with the period 1991–94 being designated the pre-reform period. They conclude that after reforms were instituted, SOBs as a whole showed no signs of becoming more sensitive to commercial criteria during the period 1995–97.

Finally, if SOBs had been transformed into independent, commercially motivated banks, their use of credit extended by the PBC should have fallen for several reasons. First, SOBs have historically had a privileged relationship with the central bank and relied heavily on cheap PBC loans to fund their own lending programs. However, as commercial banks, they would be expected to collect their own deposits and compete with other financial institutions on a level playing field. Second, in the past the government has frequently instructed the PBC to provide credit to SOBs in order to fund policy-oriented loans. As commercial banks, they would be freed of this responsibility. On this count there is some evidence that the SOBs have become more commercial in that they now do rely significantly less on PBC loans. In 1993, PBC loans accounted for 37.2 percent of total SOB loans. By 1999, this had declined to just 8.7 percent (Lardy, 1998a, p. 88; *ACFB* various years). Other sources reveal that in 1993, SOBs received 97 percent of the loans extended by the PBC to financial institutions in China. This share fell to 90 percent in 1994, 60 percent in 1995, 53.5 percent in 1996 and 39.8 percent in 1997 (*ACFB 1998*, p. 21).

THE OBJECTIVES OF STATE-OWNED BANKS

To summarize the findings of the previous section, the behavior of SOBs during the reform period, and even since their formal labeling as commercial banks in 1995, indicates that their objectives have remained considerably different to the typical commercial banking firm. An examination of the laws that have governed the activities of SOBs during the reform period is instructive in understanding the nature of this difference. It appears that the major reason the behavior of SOBs has diverged from the commercial banking firm model is that their objectives are more akin to a development bank. Diamond and Raghavan (1982, p. 33) describe the purposes of a development bank in the following way. 'The acceptance of responsibility for furthering the nation's development policies is the special factor that makes a bank a development bank. Whatever its name, that responsibility makes a conventional financial institution a development finance institution.' The objective of a development bank is to maximize the development impact of lending, subject to the necessary condition that its operations remain solvent (Bhatt, 1982, p. 61). This objective is considerably different to a commercial bank because there are often large divergences between financial and developmental returns to lending.

The objectives that SOBs have been meant to follow during the reform period are outlined in two pieces of legislation; the 1986 Interim Banking Control Regulations of the People's Republic of China (IBCR), and more recently the 1995 Commercial Banking Law of the People's Republic of China (CBL). Article 3 of the IBCR states that the activities of all financial institutions 'Shall be aimed at economic development, stabilization of currency, and promotion of beneficial social and economic results'(*ACFB 1990*,

EE, p. 177). Point 2 of Article 14 states that one of the fundamental functions of SOBs is, 'To grant loans to enterprises in line with state policies and plans'. Profitability in lending is not even mentioned as a specific objective. In the more recent CBL, SOBs are required to assume greater responsibility for their own profits and losses, and thus take into account the likelihood of repayment before extending loans (*ACFB 1996*, EE, pp. 183,189). The General Lending Rules, an order of the PBC in 1995, explicitly states that profitability is now to be used as a basic principle to guide lending (*ACFB 1996*, EE, p. 245). However, the CBL also specifies that profitability is not to be the sole criterion SOBs are to consider. Article 34 of the CBL states, 'A commercial bank shall conduct its loan business in accordance with the need for the development of the national economy and social progress and under the guidance of the state industrial policy'. Article 41 continues that, 'A commercial bank owned solely by the state should provide loans for special projects approved by the State Council'. Therefore, the objectives of SOBs are now a combination of development and commercial goals.

THE PERFORMANCE OF STATE-OWNED BANKS

The fact that SOBs were originally instituted as development banks, and continue to hold strong development-related objectives, implies that the exclusive use of commercial criteria to evaluate their performance is inappropriate. For one, profit maximization would be an inappropriate goal. All development banks, and in particular those that are state-owned, will naturally attach more importance to the development impact of their lending than financial returns. Thus, directly testing the development impact of SOB lending is a necessary addition to evaluating their performance. Second, the particular criteria that a development bank uses to evaluate potential borrowers will have a direct relationship to the development objectives of the country in which it operates (Bhatt, 1982, p. 61). As a socialist market economy, it would be naïve to presume that all of China's development objectives are financial or even economic in nature. Social goals are also considered important, and hence the extent to which SOBs have helped to facilitate these goals should be included in their performance evaluation. Finally, it is a necessary condition even for development banks that their operations remain solvent. However, the solvency of state-owned financial institutions cannot simply be assessed by comparing the value of non-performing loans (NPLs) with the value of owners' capital and loan–loss provisions specified in a balance sheet. It is necessary to consider the burden NPLs represent to the government's fiscal resources.

The Development Impact of State-Owned Bank Lending

One way a general picture of the development impact of the SOBs' lending can be gained is by comparing the productivity of aggregate investment funded through domestic loans relative to other funding sources. This approach can be applied because SOBs continue to dominate China's loans market and has already been used in several previous studies (Li, 1994; Laurenceson and Chai, 2001; Li and Liu, 2001; Liu and Li, 2001). All of these studies regressed a measure of output against the rate of investment, which in official statistics is disaggregated into that which has been funded by state budget appropriations (SBA), domestic loans (DL), foreign investment (FI) and the self-raised funds of firms (SRF). In addition to the rate of investment, previous studies have also included other explanatory variables such as labor, exports and human capital. However, with the occasional exception of exports, other variables were found to be statistically insignificant and costly in terms of degrees of freedom. Thus, the model used in this research is based on a simple aggregate production function of the Harrod–Domar type, which posits that investment is the primary driver of economic growth. Apart from reasons of simplicity and economizing on statistical degrees of freedom, the Harrod–Domar framework is a popular analytical tool for understanding economic development in countries such as China where investment in the context of a low capital–labor ratio can be expected to be the primary growth driver. Indeed, that fixed investment has been the primary driver of economic growth in China has been confirmed by two recent studies (Yu, 1998; Kwan, et al., 1999).

To model the relationship between investment disaggregated into its various funding sources and real GDP growth, an ADL approach is used as discussed in Chapter 2. In keeping with the Harrod–Domar framework, the measure of output used is the growth rate of real GDP (GDP). Official data is used over the period 1981–2000, with the starting date being dictated by data availability. All data, notes and sources are presented in the appendix (see Table A6). Table 4.1 presents the ADL model results and the associated ECM results are presented in Table 4.2.

The explanatory power of the ADL model is extremely high with an $R^2 = 0.974$. In addition, the F statistic measuring the joint significance of all regressors is statistically significant at the 1 percent level. The model also passes diagnostic tests for autocorrelation, functional form and heteroskedasticity. The error correction term in the ECM results is statistically significant at the 1 percent level, indicating that a long-run relationship exists between the variables. This is not surprising as economic theory suggests that the rate of investment will play a fundamental role in a country's economic development.

Table 4.1   ADL (2, 2, 2, 0, 1) model results, dependent variable: GDP

Coefficient	Regression estimates		Long run estimates	
	$\hat{\beta}_i$	$S_{\hat{\beta}_i}$ (*p*-value)	$\hat{\beta}_i$	$S_{\hat{\beta}_i}$ (*p*-value)
α_0	10.872	5.559 (0.098)	15.928	12.025 (0.234)
GDP_{t-1}	0.677	0.170 (0.007)		
GDP_{t-2}	−0.360	0.188 (0.104)		
SBA_t	2.071	0.832 (0.047)	1.523	0.651 (0.057)
SBA_{t-1}	2.281	1.091 (0.082)		
SBA_{t-2}	−3.310	1.033 (0.018)		
DL_t	1.882	0.577 (0.017)	3.974	1.328 (0.024)
DL_{t-1}	0.017	0.689 (0.981)		
DL_{t-2}	0.813	0.628 (0.243)		
FI_t	1.699	0.693 (0.050)	2.489	0.666 (0.010)
SRF_t	−0.791	0.283 (0.032)	−1.963	0.810 (0.052)
SRF_{t-1}	−0.548	0.280 (0.098)		

$R^2 = 0.974$
$F_{(11, 6)} = 20.069) (0.001)$

Diagnostic tests
Serial Correlation: $F_{(1, 5)} = 5.532$ (0.065)
Functional Form: $F_{(1, 5)} = 0.028$ (0.873)
Normality: $\chi^2 (2) = (NA)$
Heteroskedasticity $= F_{(1, 16)} = 0.340$ (0.568)

With respect to individual coefficients, the results indicate that investment funded through domestic loans and foreign investment exerts the most significant and positive impact on economic growth. The estimated short-run coefficient to DL is positive and significant at the 5 percent level. In the ECM results, ΔDL, the change in DL, positively impacts upon ΔGDP, the change in GDP, at the 1 percent level. The long-run coefficient to DL is the largest quantitatively and is also positive and significant at the 5 percent level. The estimated short-run coefficient to FI is positive and significant at the 5 percent level and the ECM results show that ΔFI, the change in FI, impacts upon ΔGDP at the 5 percent level. The estimated long-run coefficient to FI is smaller than DL, although it is statistically significant at the 1 percent level. Investment funded through SBA appears to have a stronger influence on output in the short run than in the long run. In the ECM results, ΔSBA, the

Table 4.2   ADL (2, 2, 2, 0, 1) model ECM results, dependent variable: ΔGDP

	Regression estimates	
Coefficient	$\hat{\beta}_i$	$S_{\hat{\beta}_i}$ (p-value)
Δα	10.872	5.559 (0.082)
ΔGDP1	0.360	0.188 (0.087)
ΔSBA	2.071	0.832 (0.034)
ΔSBA1	3.310	1.033 (0.011)
ΔDL	1.882	0.577 (0.010)
ΔDL1	−0.813	0.628 (0.227)
ΔFI	1.699	0.693 (0.037)
ΔSRF	−0.791	0.283 (0.021)
ECM_{t-1}	−0.683	0.207 (0.009)

$R^2 = 0.973$

$F_{(8, 9)} = 26.739$ (0.000)

Note: Notation is as follows: $\Delta\alpha = \alpha_t - \alpha_{t-1}$; $\Delta SBA1 = SBA_{t-1} - SBA_{t-2}$; and so on.

change in SBA, and ΔSBA1, the change in SBA lagged one period, both display a positive relationship with ΔGDP at the 5 percent level. The estimated long-run coefficient, however, is only marginally significant at the 10 percent level. The estimated coefficients to SRF are generally insignificant and/or negative.

Interpreting econometric results in the case of China requires caution due to the limited sample size. That said, in light of the above results, the preliminary conclusion can be reached that investment funded through domestic loans has been productive, at least when compared with other investment funding sources. This finding is in line with recent results obtained by Laurenceson and Chai (2001), which attempted to examine the productivity of investment funded through domestic loans using national level data, and Liu and Li (2001), which attempted to shed light on the same issue using provincial level panel data. Given the dominance of SOBs in China's loans market, this finding suggests that the development impact of their lending has been greater than is conventionally assumed. However, it should also be noted that the result could reflect the impact of growing NBFI lending. This topic will be considered in further detail in Chapter 5.

Discussing the possible micro foundations of the relatively high marginal productivity of investment funded through domestic loans now becomes important as the econometric analysis conducted above does not identify the specific channels through which this has occurred on the firm/bank level. A discussion of this nature is particularly necessary because the stylized fact of SOBs lending almost exclusively to SOEs at low interest rates, is generally regarded as clear evidence of allocative inefficiency. One channel through which SOBs may have positively influenced economic development is that they have selected relatively productive SOEs in their lending programs. Several recent empirical studies support this conclusion. Using firm-level sample survey data over the period 1980–89, Lee (1997, p. 155) found that the marginal revenue product of capital of SOEs that had borrowed funds was greater than those that had not. Cull and Xu (2000, p. 22) extended the data set until 1994 and again found a positive relationship between bank credit and firm productivity. There are several factors within China's financial reform program that have contributed to SOBs lending to relatively productive SOEs (Cull and Xu, 2000, p. 9). For one, over time banks have been given more discretionary power in their lending decisions. Second, loan officers at SOBs have been given an incentive to lend to productive SOEs by partially linking their remuneration to the financial performance of their loan portfolio. News reports of bank managers being dismissed in response to a large rise in non-performing loans at the branch they control have also become more commonplace (*Financial Times*, 22 March 1999). Third, there have been improvements in areas such as accounting and disclosure standards that have made it easier to identify productive SOEs and good credit risks.

In addition to selection factors, the positive correlation between productive SOEs and those that had borrowed funds could also be due to SOBs promoting the productivity of SOEs. In market economies banks can influence firm performance through effective corporate governance measures such as linking future credit to the performance of the firm. In the same vein, financial institutions in China could have hardened the budget constraint of SOEs and so promoted increased firm efficiency (Kueh, 1999, p. 124). The fact that loans have replaced state budgetary appropriations as the chief source of external finance for productive fixed investment during the reform period would also have placed financial institutions in a stronger position to exert corporate governance over the SOEs. However, recent empirical analyses have suggested that credit extension has not been an important channel through which corporate governance has been exerted over SOEs. Kueh's (1999, p. 143) study, for example, concluded that the replacement of state budgetary appropriations with loans during the reform period probably increased the funds available to large and medium-scale SOEs rather than hardening the budget constraint on their investment decisions. A more plausible way that SOBs have been able to positively influence the productivity of SOEs is through their interest rate policy. It is frequently assumed that the only purpose of the low interest rate policy used by SOBs is to ease the financial burden on inefficient and unprofitable SOEs. Meanwhile, the costs in terms of allocative inefficiency are held to be extremely high. However, until SOEs and SOBs face a hard budget constraint, the benefits of higher interest rates are questionable. As long as an SOE cannot go bankrupt, it will be more concerned about the availability of credit rather than its cost (Mehran et al., 1996, p. 62). Moreover, SOBs need not concern themselves with risk when lending to SOEs because the government is the effective guarantor of these loans. In this context, Zou and Sun (1996, pp. 312, 315) argue with the aid of a theoretical model that lower real interest rates can actually act as an incentive for more productive SOE investment by moderating risk and promoting greater effort on the part of management and staff.

A second channel through which SOBs may have positively impacted upon economic development is by correcting for market failure. Financial liberalization appears sound policy advice because the state does not have sufficient information to make detailed investment decisions. However, financial deregulation in a transitional environment where prices are still distorted and enterprise budget constraints remain soft does not necessarily improve investment efficiency. In fact, it may worsen it (Chai, 1998, p. 136). The effects of financial liberalization in the context of partial price reform have already been observed in China. During the financial liberalization that characterized the early stages of the reform period, SOBs began to channel credit towards areas of the economy where state control over prices was weak (World Bank, 1990, p. 33). This was a rational response given that higher output prices increased the relative profitability of these sectors. However, as a result, the rate of investment in several key sectors of the economy where prices controls remained fell significantly and they became bottlenecks to development (Chai, 1990, p. 152). To correct this lopsided investment structure, the government was forced to step up its own investments in the neglected sectors through budgetary allocations and also by tightening its grip on the SOBs' lending (Chai, 1998, p. 136).

A third way SOBs may have promoted economic development in China is that by lending predominantly to SOEs, inflationary pressures and the scope for moral hazard to occur in lending have been moderated (McKinnon, 1991, p. 117). Transitional economies typically face a deteriorating fiscal situation as their traditional tax revenue base, the remitted profits of SOEs, is eroded. This forces the government to borrow from the state banking system to meet current expenditures. China is no exception to this phenomenon. If the government is already heavily borrowing from the state banking system, this implies that there exists little room for non-inflationary bank lending to the non-state sector. Thus, the fact that the SOBs have not lent to non-state-owned enterprises could partly explain the superior performance of China compared with other transitional economies in the area of price stability. Also, because SOBs continue to possess a soft budget constraint, this implies that they may not lend responsibly to non-state-owned enterprises anyway. Moreover, even if they did have a hard budget constraint, this alone is no guarantee of sound financial and economic performance in the absence of effective prudential regulation and supervision. The experience of China's NBFIs is enlightening in this respect and will be discussed in greater depth in Chapter 5. Many NBFIs have non-state sector owners and the bulk of their lending is directed towards non-state-owned enterprises yet recent research puts the share of NPLs in many NBFIs at an equal or greater level than in SOBs (Pei, 1998, p. 333). Similarly, foreign banks, despite their short history and supposed access to superior management systems, have recorded extremely high NPL ratios. *ACFB* (*2000*, p. 137) notes that at year-end 1999, only 74.60 percent of their loans could be classified as 'normal', while 12.19 percent were classified as 'attention' loans and 13.12 percent as NPLs.

A final channel through which SOBs may have positively influenced economic development is that through their continued support of the SOEs, many positive externalities have been conferred on the non-state sector. The importance of externalities is extremely difficult to quantify, although easy to identify. Perhaps the most significant of these externalities is that the continued operation of SOEs has provided a stable environment in which the non-state sector can flourish. Given that SOEs serve both economic and social functions, their closure potentially invokes considerable economic and political instability. Such instability is rampant in economies which have adopted a big bang approach to economic transition and has seriously affected their development drives (Rana, 1995). Zhang and Yi (1997, pp. 32, 33) list several other positive externalities that the continued support of SOEs has conferred upon the non-state sector. For one, given that SOEs perform far more than just an employment role, the risk to an individual in leaving the state sector to join a non-state business operation is extremely high. By allowing unpaid leave from SOEs, the government has reduced that risk and so promoted entrepreneurial activities. Second, by maintaining SOEs the government has effectively reduced the cost of labor to the non-state sector. Since a spouse or family member of a state sector employee can stay in state-subsidized accommodation and receive other provided benefits, non-state employers need not pay an individual's entire labor cost. Third, to the extent that SOEs have been used by the government to construct infrastructure, greater levels of private sector economic activity are likely to have been facilitated (Odedokun, 1997).

State-Owned Banks and Social Objectives

In a socialist market economy such as China, social goals also feature highly in national development objectives. Given that SOBs have strong development bank characteristics, the extent to which they have promoted social goals should also be included in their performance evaluation. This chapter endeavors to focus mainly on economic issues and hence only brief comments are made. First, as was mentioned earlier, China's SOEs still form the primary social safety net in China. Therefore, by supporting SOEs, even those that may be performing poorly by financial or economic criteria, it may be considered that SOBs have met a social goal. Second, another social goal of the central government is to promote the development of China's lagging western and central regions. Provincial level loan and fixed investment data indicates that SOBs have been supportive of this policy (Table 4.3). The SOBs' loans for fixed assets, expressed as a percentage of actual fixed investment conducted, have been consistently higher in the central and western provinces of China than in the east. Over the period 1991–97, Park and Sehrt (1999) also found a strong inverse relationship between the rate of financial intermediation provided by SOBs and the level of economic development amongst Chinese provinces. This was in contrast to other financial institutions that displayed a strong, positive relationship.

Table 4.3   *State-owned bank loans for fixed assets (% of total fixed asset investment)*

	Eastern Provinces	Central/ Western Provinces
1988	28.9	39.0
1989	35.1	48.8
1990	41.6	56.9
1991	45.3	63.7
1992	39.7	62.1
1993	32.8	54.4

Note: Data refer to all SOBs. Aggregated data concerning loans for fixed assets were available only from 1988 to 1993.

Sources:
1. Loan data are from *ACFB 1991*, CE, pp. 45, 46; *1994*, pp. 439, 440.
2. Fixed Investment data are from SSB, *CSY 1989*, CE, p. 479; *1991*, p. 145; *CSY 1990*, p. 144; *1992*, p. 128; *1993*, p. 120; *1994*, p. 142.

The Solvency of State-Owned Banks

The solvency state of SOBs has come to be regarded as perhaps the most critical factor influencing whether China will successfully complete the transition to a market economy. In considering the level of NPLs in SOBs, the researcher has to make use of scattered estimates because the SOBs are still not required to publish such data in a systematic manner. Prior to the early 1990s, it is unlikely that even the SOBs themselves knew the extent of NPLs in their portfolios because no comprehensive internal audit had ever been conducted (Cheng et al., 1997, p. 207). While this situation improved during the early 1990s, prior to 1994 each SOB had its own system and standards for classifying NPLs. As a result, comparison between SOBs, and with other domestic and foreign financial institutions, would not be meaningful. Also, any attempt by each SOB to categorize the status of loans during this time was largely pointless anyway because they were only allowed to classify a certain percentage of their total loans as non-performing, irrespective of their actual status, and they were not permitted to independently write off any sizeable bad debts without the specific approval of the State Council (Lardy, 1998a, pp. 115, 118).

In 1995, the PBC set forth a new loan classification system and data regarding the extent of NPLs in SOBs began to emerge. Under this system of loan classification, NPLs were classified into three types. The first was 'past due loans', which included loans not repaid when due or not repaid after the due date has been passed. The second was 'doubtful loans', which included loans that are two or more years overdue or those loans made to a borrower who has suspended production or whose project is no longer being developed. The third was 'bad debt', which includes loans that have not been repaid after the borrower has been declared bankrupt and gone through liquidation. The earliest available authoritative source estimated that at year end 1994, 20.3 percent of the SOBs' loans were non-performing, with 11.3 percent being past due loans, 7.7 percent being doubtful loans and 1.3 percent being bad debt (Lardy, 1998a, p. 121). Furthermore, when Dai Xianglong became governor of the PBC in 1995, he stated that the level of NPLs had been rising by around 2 percent per annum in the few years prior. Thus, it can be extrapolated that the share of NPLs at year end 1993 was around 18.3 percent. The share of NPLs continued to rise and at year-end 1995 was placed at 22 percent, comprised of 12 percent past due loans, 8 percent doubtful loans and 2 percent bad debt. The total figure rose again in 1996 to 25 percent and remained at this level during 1997 (Lardy, 1998b, p. 83). Available reports suggest that the ratio sharply increased during 1998–99. For example, in discussing the performance of the newly created asset management companies, Dai Xianglong stated that the proportion of NPLs in SOBs had been reduced by 10 percent, to 25 percent by year-end

2000. This of course implies that the ratio of NPLs at year end 1999 stood at 35 percent (Lardy, 2001). The latest evidence suggests that the growth rate of the NPL ratio has finally begun to slow and even turn negative. According to PBC (2001, p. 54), the rate of growth in the NPL ratio for 2000 was 1.6 percent, considerably less than during 1998 and 1999. It has also been reported that SOBs had a net drop of 2.1 percent in their NPL ratio during the first half of 2001 (*Xinhua News Agency*, 13 July 2001). PBC (2001, p. 59) states that the objective of monetary authorities is to continue to reduce the NPL ratio by an average of 3 percent over the next few years. In addition, it is intended that in around two years, SOBs will be required to disclose the extent of their NPLs and in three to four years, all deposit-taking institutions will be subject to the disclosure standards of publicly listed firms.

Of considerable concern is that evidence has emerged which indicates that the above data based on the loan classification system adopted in 1995 substantially underestimate the extent of NPLs. The fact that this classification system varied considerably from international standards has already been noted and discussed by Lardy (1998a, pp. 116–118). Even PBC (1999, p. 26) stated that this system did not accurately reveal the level of risk associated with loans because it simply classified them according to the length of time by which they were overdue. To address this deficiency, in 1999 the PBC began trialing a new, risk-based classification system more in line with international standards, which is to be formally instituted nation-wide in 2002. In this new system, loans are classified into five categories, those being pass, special mention, substandard, doubtful and loss (*ACFB 1999*, p. 61; PBC, 1999, p. 26). The Bank of China recently disclosed that using this new system, its NPL ratio was 39 percent at year end 1999, which was 2.6 times the ratio of 15 percent reported the previous year using the old system (Lardy, 2001). However, in a speech to an international forum on the topic of NPLs in November 2001, Dai Xianglong quoted NPL data under the old system in stating that NPLs continued to amount to 26.62 percent of total SOBs loans (of which around 7 percent were bad) and that this data was 'broadly in line with result based on the five category risk based loan classification' (www.pbc.gov.cn). Such apparent contradictory statements continue to make analysing the level of NPLs in SOBs an imprecise endeavor.

Nevertheless, what is clear is that the level of NPLs in SOBs has, at least since the early 1990s, been greater than their listed capital, and that this ratio rose sharply during the mid-1990s. Table 4.4, column 4, for example, estimates that the NPL/listed capital ratio rose from 3.1 in 1993 to 6.0 in 1997, before falling to 4.7 in 1999 in response to central government capital injections. In any case, by this measure, SOBs continue to be technically insolvent. However, this is an inappropriate measure of solvency because the SOBs continued operation does not depend upon their listed

Table 4.4　Estimates of solvency in state-owned banks

	NPL (%)	Loans	Capital	NPL/Capital	NPL/GDP
1993	18.3	25 870	1 543	3.1	13.7
1994	20.3	32 828	1 831	3.6	14.3
1995	22.0	39 079	1 984	4.3	14.7
1996	25.0	47 448	2 097	5.7	17.5
1997	25.0	53 261	2 201	6.0	17.9
1998	30.0*	62 476	4 930	3.8	23.6
1999	35.0	65 820	4 890	4.7	28.1

Notes/Sources:
1.　Column 2 shows the percentage of total loans in SOBs that were non-performing. The sources are found in the text. The 1998 NPL figure is an estimate based on the average of the 1997 and 1999 figures. Column 3 shows the total loans of SOBs (ICBC, ABC, BOC, CCB). The unit is RMB 100 million. The source is Lardy, 1998a, p. 84; *ACFB* various years. Column 4 shows the paid in capital of SOBs (ICBC, ABC, BOC, CCB). The unit is 100 million RMB. The sources are Lardy, 1998a, p. 93; *ACFB* various years. Column 5 provides an estimate of the total value of NPLs relative to paid in capital. It is equal to $((1) \times (2))/(3)$.Column 6 provides an estimate of the total value of NPLs relative GDP. It is equal to $((1) \times (2))/\text{GDP}$.

capital but rather on the willingness and ability of the central government to support them. The willingness of the central government to support them emanates from the fact that they have been used as quasi fiscal agencies throughout the reform period. The need to use SOBs to fund expenditures that are typically met via the government budget in most countries has been driven by the fact that the central government has been unable to substantially reverse the declining trend in revenue as a percentage of GDP. In 1979, government revenue as a percentage of GDP stood at 28.4 percent. This declined to a low of 10.7 percent in 1995 before responding marginally to fiscal reforms that began in 1994 to rise to 15.0 percent by year-end 2000 (PBC, 2001, p. 96). This figure is not just low from a historical perspective but also by international standards. For example, even in other transitional economies such as Russia, the revenue share of GDP is around twice that of China (Lardy, 1999). The willingness of the central government to support the SOBs has also been demonstrated on numerous occasions, through the creation of the policy banks in 1994, a capital injection in 1998 and the creation of asset management companies in 2000 to deal with some of the NPLs accumulated by SOBs. Therefore, the real question now is not whether the central government is willing to support the SOBs, but rather does it have the ability to support them in order to ensure their long-term solvency.

As SOBs are owned by the central government, NPLs are a fiscal responsibility of the central government. Therefore, in determining changes in the solvency of SOBs in recent years, the relevant criterion is whether NPLs have remained at fiscally sustainable levels. Column 5 of Table 4.4 estimates that by 1999 the NPL/GDP ratio stood at around 30 percent. If one adds China's actual public and publicly guaranteed debt stocks at year end 1999 to this figure, China's true public debt stock was around 50 percent of GDP. Public debt in the US and Japan meanwhile account for around 60 percent and 125 percent of GDP, respectively. However, the key problem for China is that its low government revenue/GDP ratio and underdeveloped capital markets mean that it cannot sustain similar levels of public debt. Furthermore, China's contingent fiscal liabilities include more than just NPLs in SOBs. The Ministry of Finance is also the implicit guarantor of bonds issued by both the policy banks and the asset management companies. It can also be argued that the central government will have to take responsibility for NPLs in other financial institutions such RCCs. Finally, the central government must take responsibility for the social security system in the future. Lardy (1999) highlights a large unfunded pension debt, and the closure of SOEs at a greater rate than in the past can be expected to place a greater strain on social security expenditures. While the effect of such factors on the government's future fiscal position can only be estimated, simulations conducted by Lardy (1999) suggest that without substantial fiscal and financial reforms, the public debt/ GDP ratio will explode to around 110 percent by 2008 and likely trigger a financial sector collapse.

Based on such predictions, the possibility that SOB insolvency could sabotage China's successful transition to a market economy needs to be taken seriously. However, in determining whether these potentialities equate to an imminent financial collapse, it is important to remember four factors. First, the high level of NPLs is largely a historical legacy, the accumulated result of several decades of policy lending and a mandated inability to write off NPLs. This observation is not intended to demean the seriousness of the accumulated problem but rather to place the path to an NPL ratio in excess of 25 percent in some perspective. Second, real progress has been made in the reform of SOBs in recent years. Examples include the institutional reorganization of the PBC to minimize interference from local government officials, the firing of bank mangers found guilty of incompetence or mismanagement, the increased tendency to close loss-making SOEs, the assumption of a large proportion of NPLs by asset management companies and the streamlining of the SOBs' domestic networks in terms of branches and employees. Third, public confidence in the SOBs continues to be high and thus the risk of massive disintermediation and insolvency in the foreseeable future is slim. It is interesting to note that in response to the Asian crisis and domestic economic slowdown during 1997–99, there was actually a shift of both institutional and personal deposits from small and medium financial institutions to the SOBs (PBC, 2000, p. 15). This meant that the liquidity of non-state financial institutions fell considerably while that of the SOBs actually rose. Given that the public knows the SOBs are fully backed by the government, they are likely to be the last financial institutions driven into insolvency. Finally, there are limited alternative financial assets available for domestic savers. China's currency continues to not be freely convertible and capital account restrictions are tight. Thus, the SOBs are unlikely to experience a collapse in liquidity due to capital outflow of the kind experienced by many Asian banks during 1997.

CONCLUSION

While China's SOBs may be labeled commercial in name, the analysis of their behavior and objectives conducted at the beginning of this chapter showed that they also possess strong development bank characteristics. As a result, the exclusive use of commercial criteria to evaluate their performance is inadequate. When their performance evaluation is supplemented by considering the development impact of their lending and the extent to which they have met social objectives, the findings, although preliminary in nature, are more positive. The solvency state of SOBs is a serious concern in light of projections that suggest that, left unchanged, the central government's long-term fiscal position is unsustainable. However, this also needs to be tempered with the understanding that the likelihood of collapse in the short and medium term is limited.

By way of conclusion, it should be stated that the results of Chapters 3 and 4 do not imply that the economic performance of China's SOBs and SOEs, or that the level of government intervention in the financial sector more generally, has been optimal. SOBs and SOEs continue to lag well behind international best practices and numerous examples of economic inefficiency can be cited. However, the results have highlighted the transitional nature of China's economy and the crucial need to evaluate the performance of SOBs and SOEs directly and through the use of appropriate criteria.

5. Non-bank financial institutions and economic development in China

INTRODUCTION

In considering the nature of financial reform in China, and in assessing its impact on economic development, the stylized fact of SOBs lending predominantly to SOEs has attracted the overwhelming majority of research attention. It is, therefore, often assumed that the formal financial sector has played an insignificant role in facilitating the development of China's rapidly emerging non-state sector. However, as noted by Girardin and Bazen (1998, p. 141), this view could be misleading because it fails to consider the role potentially played by NBFIs. During the reform period, three types of NBFIs have risen to prominence; RCCs, UCCs and TICs.[1] Table 5.1 shows their share of China's total loans and deposits markets. The rising prominence of NBFIs in the loans market is particularly striking. In 1978 they provided just 2.4 percent of the total loans extended by financial institutions in China. By 1996, this had risen to 18.2 percent. In large part due to the increased prominence of NBFIs, the PBC's credit registration system showed that at year-end 2000, the loan balance holdings of the non-state sector was 48 percent of the total (PBC, 2001, p. 39). These data are in contrast to the popular view that China's financial system simply channels the savings of the household sector to the state enterprise sector. Thus, the scope for NBFIs to impact upon economic development has been considerable.

In light of the rapid growth that NBFIs have experienced, the objectives of this chapter are twofold. First, given that NBFIs have been marginalized in the existing literature, it aims to contribute to the understanding of NBFI development during the reform period. Second, it aims to assess the impact NBFIs have had on China's economic development. The chapter begins by providing an overview of NBFI development in China, which is then followed by a discussion concerning their ownership, control and industrial structure. The impact NBFIs can have on economic development is then reviewed briefly from a theoretical perspective before considering the case of China. Investigating the development impact of NBFIs in China does not readily lend itself to formal econometric methods because complete data sets

Table 5.1   The development of non-bank financial institutions in China

	Institutions	Loans		Deposits	
1978	RCCs	45	(2.4)	166	(12.8)
1986	RCCs	569	(6.8)	962	(14.8)
	UCCs	20	(0.2)	30	(0.5)
	TICs	218	(2.6)	130	(2.0)
1996	RCCs	6 365	(10.4)	8 794	(12.8)
	UCCs	2 445	(4.0)	3 998	(5.8)
	TICs	2 337	(3.8)	2 475	(3.6)
2001	RCCs	12 000	(11.0)	17 300	(12.0)
	UCCs				
	TICs				

Notes:
1. The unit for all data is RMB100 million. The figures in brackets are as a percent of total financial institution intermediation.
2. 1986 is the first year for which consolidated data on UCCs and TICs is available.
3. A blank space indicates that data was unavailable.

Sources:
1. *ACFB 1990*, CE, pp. 48, 65; *1997*, p. 465.
2. *ACFB 1991*, pp. 89,109–113.
3. *Zhongguo Jinrong*, various issues.
4. *Xinhua News Agency*, 2 April 2002.

of sufficient length or detail are unavailable. Nevertheless, available data are drawn upon to make an assessment.

THE DEVELOPMENT OF NON-BANK FINANCIAL INSTITUTIONS IN CHINA

According to Chandavarkar (1992, p. 135), the nature of the development of financial institutions and markets apart from the formal banking system can be classified as being either autonomous or reactive. Autonomous development refers to traditional non-bank arrangements that predate the banking system of modern times. Reactive development on the other hand refers to financial structures that develop primarily in response to controls over, or deficiencies in, the banking system.

RCCs are the only NBFI in China to have operated during the pre-reform era and have continued to be the major NBFI during the reform period. In theory, RCCs are collectively owned cooperative financial institutions that operate independently and according to democratic management principles (*ACFB 1990*, p. 80). The development of RCCs was initially promoted by the central government in the early 1950s to assist in the mobilization of rural savings and, along with the mutual aid cooperative for production, and the rural supply and marketing cooperative for the distribution of produce, promote rural development at the grass roots level (Dipchand et al., 1994, pp. 95–97). Despite their collective roots, RCCs have actually held very little autonomy and for most of their history have been run as the lowest level of state financial administration in the rural sector (Tam, 1988, p. 71). Table 5.2 presents summary data concerning the development and operation of RCCs during the reform period. It shows that while RCCs have experienced considerable development in terms of financial intermediation, the number of RCCs has actually undergone consolidation, falling particularly in recent years. This has primarily been due to the closure or merger of insolvent RCCs by

Table 5.2   Summary rural credit cooperative data

	1978	1985	1990	1995	1999
Total assets		956	2 999		14 300
Total loans	45	400	1 413	5 234	9 226
Agricultural collectives	22	41	134	1 095	
Township enterprises	12	164	761	2 779	
Farmer households	11	194	518	1 360	
Total deposits	166	725	2 145	7 173	13 358
Agricultural collectives		88	150		
Township enterprises		72	153		
Farmer households	56	565	1 842	6 196	
Paid in capital		32	82	378	654
Institutions		58 603	58 200	20 219	39 516

Note:
1.   The unit for all financial data is RMB100 million.
2.   A blank space indicates that data was unavailable.

Sources:
1.   *ACFB* various years
2.   PBC, *CFO* various years
3.   CMS, 1996 (7), p. 54.

the PBC. In 1998 alone, the number of RCCs with legal person status was reduced by 5953 (*ACFB 1999*, p. 163).

UCCs emerged as the urban counterparts to RCCs during the reform period. However, in contrast to RCCs, the initial formation of UCCs was more independent of the policies of the central government. UCCs emerged in a reactive fashion in order to meet the financial needs of the emerging urban non-state sector that was not well served by the SOBs. Non-state sector agents often experienced considerable difficulty in undertaking even basic financial transactions such as opening bank accounts, depositing and borrowing funds, and settling accounts through the SOBs (Dipchand et al., 1994, p. 101). In response to such difficulties the first UCC emerged in 1979. They developed rapidly in spite of the fact that official legislation enabling their formation did not emerge until 1986. According to Table 5.3, which provides summary data on the development of UCCs, by this time their number had already reached 1 114. It was not until 1989 that national level regulations governing the operations of UCCs were issued. Prior to this time, there were at least 11 different local regulations (Girardin and Xie, 1997, pp. 41, 42).

Table 5.3   Summary urban credit cooperative data

	1986	1990	1995	1998
Total assets	32	372	4 545	2 673
Total loans	20	249	1 929	1 690
Collectively owned firms	13	161	1 080	
Individual proprietors	2	25	156	
Other loans	4	63	693	
Total deposits	30	310	3 357	2 462
Collectively owned firms	18	100	872	
Individual proprietors	4	17	141	
Individual savings and other	8	93	2 344	
Paid in capital	1.4	28.2	136.0	273.9
Institutions	1 114	3 421	5 104	3 240

Notes:
1.   The unit for all financial data is RMB100 million.
2.   Aggregated data for UCCs began in 1986.

Sources:
1.   *ACFB* various years
2.   PBC, various years
3.   CMS, 1996 (7), p. 55.

Official acceptance and a period of economic expansion saw the number of UCCs further triple by 1988. Inflation then became a serious problem for the Chinese economy and monetary authorities largely placed the blame on excessive lending by financial institutions. As a result, the PBC instigated a financial sector rectification program that dramatically slowed the licensing of new UCCs (Girardin and Xie, 1997, p. 41). The rectification program ended in early 1992 and UCCs experienced a new surge in growth increasing to 5 229 by 1994 (PBC, 1996, p. 100). More recently, based largely on solvency concerns, the PBC has encouraged consolidation amongst UCCs. Numerous individual UCCs have been merged to form Urban Cooperative Banks, which are profit motivated financial institutions that are intended to provide greater competition for SOBs in urban areas (PBC, 1998, p. 30). For example, in early 1996 the Beijing Urban Cooperative Bank was formed from the merger of 90 local UCCs (Lardy, 1998a, p. 72). By 1997, 61 such banks had opened for business (*ACFB 1998*, pp. 120–124). Other UCCs are currently being required to return to their cooperative roots, with their management being transferred to RCC unions in their locality (*ACFB 2000*, p. 142).

The initial formation of TICs could be classified as reactive in that in 1980 the central government actively encouraged the SOBs to establish trust and investment departments in order to promote a more horizontal flow of funds in China's financial sector. Under China's pre-reform monetary system, funds simply moved vertically from the PBC to SOEs. This flow of funds became unsuitable after reforms began because credit only flowed to those firms under the national plan and any surplus state funds lay idle. In addition to SOBs, numerous other organizations such as provincial and local level governments and even some enterprises set up their own TICs. By 1981 there were 620 TICs in China (Dipchand et al., 1994, p. 104). The reason for their rapid development can also be attributed to reactive factors, although different to those that were responsible for their initial formation. The reason TICs were viewed so attractively by their sponsors was because they were only loosely regulated and could often be used as a means of overcoming central government controls over the banking system. For example, it became common practice for SOBs that were nearing their annual credits limit to refer a potential client to their associated TIC (Dipchand et al., 1994, p. 110). Also, as the share of central government budgetary expenditures for investment declined during the reform period, and the SOBs lending was restricted by the credit plan, local governments increasingly looked to TICs to raise funds for local investment. Some commentators have gone so far as to say that TICs have become the 'treasury arms of local government' (*The Economist*, 16 January 1999).

Kumar et al. (1997, p. 3) states that the central authorities sought to control the development of TICs on four occasions, mainly in response to inflationary pressures bought on by a rapid increase in lending outside of the credit plan. The first attempt was in 1982 when the ownership of TICs was restricted to SOBs and a few selected local governments (Dipchand et al., 1994, p. 105). When this proved ineffective a second attempt was made by the PBC in 1986 that required SOBs to shift their trust and investment business to a separate entity so that it could be monitored more effectively. This, however, did not slow their growth in number and by 1988 there were 745 PBC approved TICs, although unofficially it was thought to be closer to 1000 (Kumar et al., 1997, p. 3). The financial sector rectification program of the late 1980s represented the third attempt to control the development of TICs and was characterized by considerable consolidation. By year-end 1990 the number of TICs had been more than halved to 339. After this program ended, TICs again began to experience growth in terms of number and volume of lending. In 1994, there were renewed concerns that leakages from the credit plan had been funding uncontrolled investment and inflation. There were also concerns that some TICs had begun to engage in a range of unauthorized activities. Therefore, in 1995 all TICs were required to reregister with the PBC in order to weed out offending institutions. This latest govern-

Table 5.4   Summary trust and investment company data

	1986	1990	1995	1999
Total assets	292	1 181	4 586	6 323
Total loans	218	891	2 410	
Entrusted loans	69	417	1 462	
Trust loans	85	321	694	
Other loans	64	153	254	
Total deposits	130	674	2 499	
Entrusted deposits	81	457	1 677	
Trust deposits	40	154	625	
Other deposits	8	63	197	
Paid in capital	72.9	263.2	449.4	
Institutions		339	330	239

Notes:
1. The unit for all financial data is RMB100 million.
2. Aggregated data for TICs began in 1986.

Sources:
1. *ACFB*, various years
2. PBC, various years

ment initiative meant that by 1999 the number of TICs had been reduced to 239 with plans for further consolidation ahead (PBC, 2000, p. 22)

OWNERSHIP, CONTROL AND INDUSTRIAL STRUCTURE OF NON-BANK FINANCIAL INSTITUTIONS

RCCs are owned by shareholders that are typically non-state sector rural households. In the early 1970s it was estimated that more than 90 percent of rural households held some equity stock in RCCs (Yi ,1994, p. 254). As cooperative institutions, the control of RCCs has always nominally rested with shareholders and their primary purpose has been to provide financial services to these members, as opposed to implementing the state plan like SOBs, or chasing profits like commercial financial institutions. However, despite their ownership stake, the control of RCCs has never really rested with rural households. Rather, up until recently RCCs have been subject to the supervision of the ABC, which in actual fact consisted of a host of direct controls over their operations. Also, because RCCs were effectively incorporated into the state financial system, local governments have been able to gain a degree of control over their operations (Zhu et al., 1997, pp. 80–81). This is because under the decentralization of financial resources and decision-making authority that took place during the early years of economic reform, local branches of state-owned financial institutions were effectively placed under the control of local government (Wu, 1995, p. 95). Specific controls placed on RCCs have included extremely high reserve ratio requirements, restrictions over the volume, direction and pricing of credit, and a loss of autonomy with respect to senior staffing decisions (Tam, 1988, p. 72; World Bank, 1990, p. 12; Huang, 1995, p. 135). It was not until the mid-1990s that several concrete steps were taken to restore the independence of RCCs. First, in 1994 the government established the Agricultural Development Bank of China to fund all rural policy related activities, and so freed the RCCs of the need to assist in this task (PBC, 1995, p. 51). Second, in 1996 the subordinate position of the RCCs with respect to the ABC was officially severed and they, like all other financial institutions in China, were placed under the direct supervision of the PBC (*ACFB 1998*, EE, p. 37).

The industrial structure of individual RCCs is of low concentration because they are single office entities with the only branching permitted being small, often part-time, credit stations. In 1997, the average value of assets held by individual RCCs was RMB28.7 million, which meant that on average their scale was slightly larger than individual branches of the ABC (*ACFB 1998*, EE, p. 195; *ACFB 1998*, CE, pp. 652, 653). Sample surveys reveal also that there are large-scale differences depending upon the RCCs' location. For

example, Tam (1988, p. 73) cites Chinese research that showed average outstanding loan balances of RCCs located in western China were only 17
percent of those located in eastern provinces.

UCCs are owned exclusively by non-state sector shareholders, which generally consist of a diversified group of collectively-owned enterprises,
privately-owned enterprises, individual proprietors and urban residents, excluding government officials (*ACFB 1990*, EE, p. 83; Girardin and Xie, 1997,
p. 63). The daily control of a UCC rests with a management council that is
democratically elected at an annual meeting of shareholders. Unlike other
financial institutions in China, local governments have rarely interfered in the
operations of individual UCCs (Girardin and Xie, 1997, p. 66). There are
several reasons for this. First, their lending is already focused on a particular
locality and hence local governments do not need to be concerned that funds
will flow out to competing areas. Second, individual UCCs are relatively
small in scale and hence their ability, especially when compared with SOBs,
to fund major urban developments is limited. Third, since 1989 no government agency has been able to hold an ownership stake in a UCC, nor have
full-time government officials been permitted to hold employment positions
(Girardin and Xie, 1997, pp. 52, 53).

The industrial structure of individual UCCs is of low concentration because they are single office entities with the only branching permitted being
small UCC affiliates which act on behalf of a UCC in a location where it may
not otherwise be represented (Girardin and Xie, 1997, p. 38). In 1996, the
average value of assets held by individual UCCs was RMB122 million,
which meant that on average their scale was slightly larger than individual
branches of the ICBC, the dominant SOB in urban areas (*ACFB 1998*, EE,
p. 194; *ACFB 1997*, CE, pp. 591, 592). As with RCCs, sample survey evidence reveals considerable scale differences depending upon the locality in
which the UCC operates (Girardin and Xie, 1997, p. 65).

Unlike RCCs and UCCs, most TICs are owned by state agencies. In 1982,
SOBs owned 92 percent of TICs (Kumar et al., 1997, p. 8). This share
declined throughout the 1980s as more local governments established their
own TIC (Lardy, 1998a, p. 73). By 1994, only 47 percent of TICs were
affiliated with SOBs and they only controlled 6.4 percent of total TIC assets
(Kumar et al., 1997, p. 11). This declining trend continued with the introduction of the new commercial banking law in 1995 that required SOBs to divest
themselves of all affiliation with trust and investment business. PBC (1998,
p. 270) states that this divestiture process had been completed by year end
1997.

Even though in the past SOBs have possessed a sizeable ownership stake
in TICs, it is local governments that have always held the real control over
their operations. This is because local branches of SOBs have generally been

subject to the authority of local governments. Therefore, TICs owned by SOBs, in addition to those directly owned by local governments, were also under pressure to fund the pet projects of local administrators (Dipchand et al., 1994, p. 110).

Despite the fact that TICs are many in number, trust and investment business in China is quite highly concentrated. The concentration has grown in recent years with new rounds of consolidation. China International Trust and Investment Corporation (CITIC) is by far the largest TIC. In 1988, when there were 745 TICs, CITIC held assets worth RMB65 billion, or 26 percent of total TIC assets (Kumar et al., 1997, p. 10). By 1997, CITIC held assets worth RMB221 billion, or 51 percent of total TIC assets (*ACFB 1997*, CE, p. 603; PBC, 1998, p. 33). Several provincial level TICs are also extremely large. For example, in 1994 when there were 391 TICs, the combined assets of the three largest provincial TICs amounted to RMB50 billion, or 13 percent of total TIC assets. The smallest TIC at this time held assets worth RMB68 million (Kumar et al., 1997, p. 9).

THE IMPACT OF NON-BANK FINANCIAL INSTITUTIONS ON ECONOMIC DEVELOPMENT IN CHINA

The theoretical literature suggests that NBFIs (and informal credit markets) can impact upon economic development in numerous ways. On a positive note, NBFIs can boost savings mobilization over and above that which can be achieved via a banking system alone. This is possible for two reasons. First, NBFIs are generally not subject to the interest rate controls frequently imposed on banks in developing countries. Second, because NBFIs are more flexible in organizational structure and local in focus, they are more willing and able to provide a deposit collection service where banks could not profitably do so. NBFIs can also promote economic development by improving the efficiency with which investible funds are allocated in the economy. NBFIs accomplish this primarily by servicing the credit needs of borrowers that are excluded from accessing the banking system. Banking systems may exclude some borrowers that have access to high return investments for two reasons. First, because the lending of banks in developing countries is often directed in part by the government, they are forced to ration credit in favor of some borrowers to the exclusion of others. Second, it is well known that due to the effects of imperfect and costly information, even liberalized banking systems will ration credit in favor of large-scale borrowers that can either offer collateral or provide documented credit references (Tsang, 1995, p. 847). NBFIs can alleviate these deficiencies because (a) their lending operations are subject to fewer controls, and (b) they are able to better deal with problems of imperfect information because they have superior local information and can devise alternative monitoring and collateral arrangements such as the linking of credit extension to marketing, employment or leasing transactions (Stiglitz, 1990; Ghate, 1992; Banerjee et al., 1994).

It should be noted, however, that the impact NBFIs have on economic development is not unanimously positive from a theoretical perspective. Girardin and Bazen (1998, p. 143), for example, note that because NBFIs are subject to fewer controls than banks, they often tend to operate on the fringes of even prudential regulation and supervision. This means that NBFIs can be vulnerable to engaging in excessively risky activities. Thus, to evaluate the sustainability of the NBFIs' influence on economic development, it is important to assess their solvency status. The fact that NBFI lending is often not subject to formal controls can also mean that they can have a negative influence on macroeconomic stability and frustrate monetary policy. Thus, gauging the effects of NBFIs in this area should also form part of their performance evaluation.

With respect to raising funds for investment, the performance of NBFIs in China has been impressive, particularly with respect to mobilizing savings in rural areas. Table 5.5, for example, compares the non-state sector savings mobilization performance of RCCs with that of the ABC, the largest SOB in rural areas. Unfortunately, disaggregated non-state sector data are available from the balance sheet of the ABC only during the years of 1985–90. Never-

Table 5.5   Non-state sector rural savings mobilization

	ABC			RCCs	
Year	TE	CF and FH		TE	CF and FH
1985	31	7		72	637
1986	46	10		92	850
1987	54	12		105	1 096
1988	62	15		128	1 241
1989	56	17		126	1 504
1990	66	19		150	1 948

Notes:
1.   All data are in units of RMB100 million.
2.   TE: Township enterprises, CF: Collective farming, FH: Farm households.

Sources:
1.   *ACFB* 1991, p. 94
2.   SSB, 1996, p. 617.

theless, the available data clearly show that RCCs mobilized far more savings from various non-state sector units such as township enterprises, collective farming and farm households. The savings mobilization performance of RCCs is particularly important for several reasons. First, as noted earlier, servicing the non-state sector has been a deficiency of the state banking system. Thus, RCCs have helped to alleviate this shortcoming. Second, the geographically dispersed nature of such rural non-state savers, and their individually small level of surplus, often means that they are not serviced by the banking system in many developing countries. By the 1990s, RCCs had collectively become the second largest holder of individual savings deposits in China, behind only the ICBC (Watson, 1998, p. 32).

The influence of NBFIs on the allocative efficiency of capital appears to have been positive for RCCs and UCCs, while being limited or even negative in the case of TICs. This is because RCCs and UCCs have serviced the credit needs of non-state sector borrowers that had previously been largely excluded from accessing credit from the SOBs. Table 5.2 showed that RCCs have lent predominantly to agricultural collectives, township enterprises and farmer households. Similarly, Table 5.3 showed that UCCs have focused on the urban non-state sector including collectively owned firms and individual proprietors. This conclusion is supported by Girardin and Xie's (1997, p. 64) sample survey of UCCs in 1994, which estimated that 78.8 percent of UCC credit was extended to non-state borrowers. It is useful to place the non-state sector lending of RCCs and UCCs in a comparative perspective to gauge its importance. Table 5.6 uses balance sheet data to compare the loans extended by RCCs and the ABC to various non-state sector rural borrowers. As was the case with Table 5.5, disaggregated non-state sector data for the ABC are available only during the years 1985–90. The data show that while initially the ABC extended more loans to township enterprises and collective farming, by the end of the period the RCCs lending to these units had surpassed that of the ABC. Furthermore, the lending of RCCs to farm households far eclipsed that of the ABC over the entire period. Watson (1998, p. 32) reports that RCCs provide about 80 percent of total peasant household borrowing. *ACFB 2000* (p. 145) states that in 1999 RCC loans to agriculture and township and village enterprises accounted for 63.4 percent and 68.0 percent of total financial sector loans to these recipients respectively. Available data also indicate that over time UCCs have become a more important source of credit for urban, non-state sector borrowers than the SOBs. Table 5.7, for example, compares the lending of UCCs and SOBs with respect to various non-state sector borrowers. Unfortunately, comparable data are available only for a few years. Nevertheless, they indicate that by 1996, the UCCs loans to urban and township collective enterprises were 20 percent greater than those extended by SOBs, and those to individual proprietors were nearly 300 percent greater.

Table 5.6   Lending to the rural non-state sector

	ABC			RCCs		
	CF	TE	FH	CF	TE	FH
1985	66	188	54	41	164	194
1986	65	288	64	45	266	258
1987	72	350	79	65	359	348
1988	83	408	87	80	456	372
1989	96	421	91	107	572	416
1990	114	462	99	134	761	518

Notes:
1.   All data are in units of RMB100 million.
2.   CF: Collective farming, TE: Township enterprises, FH: Farm households.

Sources:
1.   *ACFB* 1991, p. 93
2.   SSB, 1996, p. 617.

Table 5.7   Lending to the urban non-state sector

	SOBs		UCCs	
	UTE	IP	UTE	IP
1994	1 142	54	929	101
1995	1 066	34	1 080	156
1996	1 200	54	1 439	213

Notes:
1.   All data are in units of RMB100 million.
2.   UTE: Urban and township enterprises, IP: Individual proprietors.

Sources:
1.   PBC, 1994, p. 94
2.   *ACFB 1996*, p. 122; *ACFB 1997*, CE, p. 465.

Thus, while the overall amount of loans extended by RCCs and UCCs remains smaller than the SOBs, their significance to the non-state sector has been considerably more important.

The allocative efficiency impact of TICs is less impressive for two reasons. First, their involvement with the non-state sector has been considerably less than RCCs and UCCs. Second, it has been widely recognized, including by the PBC, that a significant proportion of their lending has been allocated to unproductive and unauthorized investment activities such as excessive property development and financial market speculation (PBC, 1994, p. 32; *ACFB 1997*, EE, p. 46).

In evaluating the impact NBFIs have had on non-state sector development, it is also important to consider the role played by the informal credit market. This is because it has been shown that in many developing countries the informal credit market has also been an important supplier of credit to the non-state sector (Roemer, 1986; Ghate, 1992). Numerous sample surveys have revealed the existence of a large informal credit market in China (Tam, 1991, pp. 516–517). It has been estimated that around one half of all rural credit is extended through informal channels, such as from relatives and friends (Feder et al., 1993, p. 111). However, despite the vast size of the informal financial sector, sample survey evidence suggests that it has not substituted for the role played by NBFIs as the financial engine of growth behind the rapidly developing non-state sector. This is because credit extended by RCCs and UCCs is used almost exclusively for production-related activities, while informal credit is generally used to fund personal consumption, conventional social expenditures such as weddings and funerals, and residential construction (Manoharan, 1992, pp. 206–207; Feder et al., 1993, p. 119; Zhu et al., 1997, pp. 104, 105; Girardin and Xie, 1997, p. 64).

As noted in the theoretical review, in evaluating the impact of NBFIs on economic development it is also important to investigate whether the prudential framework surrounding them has been sufficient to ensure their solvency. The state of the regulatory framework governing the management of NBFIs has varied considerably between institutions and over time. For example, RCCs have long been subject to controls over their operations that have extended well beyond that which could be justified on prudential grounds. In contrast, at least during the initial stages of their development, UCCs and TICs operated on the fringes of even prudential regulation. Over time, prudential regulation of NBFIs has also become more indirect in nature and in line with international regulatory standards. For example, even though rudimentary asset–liability management principles for UCCs were first introduced in 1989, the PBC at this time still chiefly controlled their operations through direct controls such as credit ceilings (Girardin and Xie, 1997, pp. 49, 51). However, in 1994 credit ceilings were replaced with a more detailed system of asset–liability management principles governing capital adequacy, asset liquidity and risk exposure. This new system was more in keeping with international norms requiring, for example, that UCCs maintain a capital to asset ratio of at least 8 percent. Asset–liability principles were also issued in 1994 for TICs. Kumar et al. (1997, p. 31) contends that the asset–liability ratios imposed on TICs may actually be more comprehensive than those that have been imposed on NBFIs in mature market economies.

However, while the state of the regulatory framework governing the management of NBFIs has improved significantly, available data suggest that the PBC's supervisory success in ensuring regulatory compliance and solvency has been modest. On a positive note, the results of Girardin and Xie's (1997, p. 68) 1994 sample survey indicated that UCCs were generally solvent in that NPLs were less than self-owned funds. Girardin and Xie (1997, p. 42) further add that through 1995 only 133 UCCs had been either abolished or merged as a result of solvency issues. This was not particularly high given that the total number of UCCs in 1995 was greater than 5000. However, it should be noted that the reliability of the feedback provided by UCCs in the above sample survey is questionable. For example, the sample survey indicated that only 4.7 percent of UCC loans were non-performing. Pei (1998, p. 333) meanwhile cites other Chinese research that places their level at around 20–30 percent of total loans. Furthermore, Liu (1999, p. 299) reports that of the 42 problem depository institutions that were closed during 1997–98 by the PBC for solvency reasons, 23 were UCCs.

However, whatever the solvency status of UCCs, there is little doubt that RCCs and TICs have fared worse. In 1990 it was reported that up to 40 percent of RCCs were making losses (Watson, 1998, p. 29). At the time of their de-linking from the ABC at year-end 1996, NPL's accounted for 38 percent of total loans (up from 30.5 percent the year before) and 53 percent of RCCs were losing money. Even without deducting bad loans from the assets of RCCs, by year-end 1999 their total losses amounted to RMB 86.2 billion, resulting in net assets of negative 8.1 billion RMB (Zuo, 2001). PBC (2001, p. 57) acknowledges that in 2000 RCCs as a whole were still incurring losses. The primary reason for the RCCs poor financial performance can be traced back to their subordinate relationship to the ABC and the numerous controls that have been placed on their operations (Tam, 1988, p. 72; Watson, 1998, p. 27). Their close connection to the state financial system also meant that many local governments felt no compulsion to repay loans because they considered such transactions as being 'from the public, to the public' (Zhu et al., 1997, p. 80).

The regulatory compliance of TICs has been so poor that on several occasions the PBC has resorted to temporarily suspending all trust and investment business (Dipchand et al., 1994, p. 105). It also appears that the compliance of TICs worsened during the 1990s as they became increasingly involved in high risk, unauthorized activities such as financial market speculation and real estate development (Kumar et al., 1997, p. 15). NPLs have been placed at 30–50 percent of total TIC loans (Pei, 1998, p. 333). According to the data in Table 5.4, this implies that TICs taken as a whole are also technically insolvent with NPLs far in excess of paid-in capital. These events have forced the PBC to close or merge several TICs in recent years, with the most notable being Guangdong International Trust and Investment Corporation (GITIC) in October 1998. GITIC's experience is typical of many TICs in China during the 1990s, and indeed the wider experience of many NBFIs throughout Asia. It experienced rapid asset growth to become the largest NBFI in Guangdong province, and second only among all TICs in China to the central government run CITIC (*Xinhua News Agency*, 29 January 1999; van Kemenade, 1999, p. 171). GITIC fuelled this asset expansion in recent years by borrowing heavily from overseas sources, accumulating $US1.2 billion in registered foreign currency borrowings (*Time International*, 1 February 1999). In addition, it has been reported that it was able to utilize its close links with Hong Kong to obtain far more foreign funds without proper central government authorization (van Kemenade, 1999, p. 171). Many of these loans were short term in maturity and incurred high rates of interest. To repay them GITIC participated in speculative ventures such as property market investment to the extent that it became the largest real estate developer in southern China (*The Economist*, 16 January 1999). The property bubble in China eventually burst and when GITIC was finally closed it was left with a balance sheet that revealed liabilities worth $US4.4 billion and assets worth just $US2.6 billion (*Time International*, 1 February 1999). Moral hazard and inadequate supervision are the primary factors driving excessive risk taking amongst TICs. Since most TICs are either directly owned or controlled by some level of government, any losses are generally borne by the state rather than by management. Furthermore, due to a shortage of resources available to the PBC to supervise TICs, some have only been subject to an on-site inspection once every three to four years (Kumar et al., 1997, pp. 34, 53).

The performance of NBFIs with respect to their influence on macroeconomic stability is also of concern. The PBC has blamed inflationary episodes during the reform period chiefly on rapid credit creation by financial institutions outside of the credit plan. Given that SOBs were formally subject to credit ceilings until 1998 (although these were not always strictly enforced), much of this excessive lending was extended via NBFIs. As a result, the development of NBFIs has mirrored the business cycle, experiencing rapid growth during periods of economic expansion before undergoing consolidation as part of the PBC's attempts to control inflation.

CONCLUSION

The conclusion that the formal financial sector in China has not supported the rapid growth in the non-state sector during the reform period is premature until the role played by NBFIs is considered. Available data suggest that NBFIs have been an important channel through which non-state sector savings have been mobilized. RCCs in particular have been successful in extending the reach of the formal financial sector to areas where the banking system would not have found it viable to do so. The influence of NBFIs with respect to contributing to an efficient allocation of loanable funds also appears to have been positive on the whole, with RCCs and UCCs providing the financial engine of growth behind the non-state sector during the reform period. On a less positive note, the sustainability of the NBFIs' impact on economic development is questionable due to serious solvency concerns. While the regulatory framework surrounding NBFIs has improved, adequate supervision to ensure compliance with regulations continues to be lacking. Also, the fact that NBFIs have frequently been used by banks and local governments to circumvent central government controls, along with the fact that the development of NBFIs has tended to mirror the business cycle, indicates that their impact on macroeconomic stability has been dubious.

NOTE

1. Other NBFIs have also emerged that include finance companies, insurance companies, the postal savings network and quasi formal institutions such as rural cooperative funds. These however are not discussed here for reasons of space.

6. Stock markets and economic development in China

INTRODUCTION

The focus of the preceding discussion has been on issues with respect to credit markets. However, an analysis of financial reform and economic development in China would be incomplete without devoting specific attention to China's stock markets. The promotion of stock markets in China has received considerable support from many economists for two key reasons. First, stock markets are seen by some as a means of overcoming the negative effects of financial repression in China's credit markets (Li, 1994, p. 3). For example, if a privately owned firm could not gain access to credit from the state banking system, then an equity issue could represent a viable alterative investment funding source. Cho (1986) takes this argument one step further by contending that even with fully liberalized credit markets, equity markets are an essential component to an efficient financial system due to their ability to alleviate the intrinsic market failures suffered by credit markets. Second, others see stock markets as an 'indispensible' means of reforming China's large SOEs (Xiang, 1998). According to this view, transforming SOEs into shareholding companies can provide them with the necessary funds to modernize, reduce their dependence upon debt finance and improve corporate governance.

However, other economists have criticized the view that China should promote the stock market (Singh, 1990; He, 1994). Such writers often point to the successful bank-based development experiences of countries such as Germany and Japan, and on this basis argue that stock markets are not necessary institutions for achieving high levels of economic development and that China would be better off concentrating on reforming the existing banking system. The intrinsic problems of stock markets, such as their proneness to high degrees of volatility, are also common arguments presented by those not in favor of their increased promotion.

While there is considerable debate on the appropriate standing that stock markets should be given in China, there has been very little work done examining their impact on economic development to date. Therefore, this chapter aims to undertake such an analysis. The theory of stock market development is first briefly reviewed before considering the nature and extent of equity issues and stock market development in China. Some of the key theoretical and empirical contributions on the effects of stock markets on economic development are then reviewed. Finally, available data are used to investigate the effects stock markets have had on economic development in China.

STOCK MARKET DEVELOPMENT IN CHINA

A Descriptive Overview of Stock Market Development

Various studies (see Demirguc-Kunt and Levine, 1996 for a review) have shown that as economies develop, investment financing tends to evolve from self-finance, to intermediated debt finance and finally to direct capital markets for debt and equity. Thus, there are some factors endogenous to the process of economic development that encourage the issuance of equity and the formation of stock markets. These include an increased need to access external funding to finance large-scale investment, rising disposable incomes and a desire to better manage risk (McKinnon, 1973; Jensen and Meckling, 1976; He, 1994, pp. 194–198). However, other authors have noted that this typical progression has not taken place in a number of developed countries (Singh and Weiss, 1998, p. 618). Thus, stock market development also appears to depend upon a set of factors that are exogenous to the process of economic development. Central to these factors is the role played by government, including the favored system of corporate governance, whether an effective prudential framework surrounding stock markets can be installed and whether the banking system is heavily repressed (Stiglitz, 1994, p. 21; Mayer, 1994, p. 182).

The stock market in China has undergone two, quite distinct, stages of development. The first stage ran from 1980–90, while the second stage began in 1991 and continues until the present. Data on equity issues and stock markets during the first stage of development are scarce (Table 6.1). One of the main reasons for this, and a distinguishing feature of this initial stage of development, is that they experienced the wavering support of the central government. Tam (1991, p. 518) contends that most share issues during this initial stage were marketed informally and were never reported to any monitoring agencies. Initially, central government support wavered on the basis of concerns over whether shares were consistent with socialist ownership principles. Therefore, while shares first emerged in 1980, they were primarily confined to funding non-state sector companies and projects sponsored by local governments. It was not until mid-1984 that share issues were featured

Table 6.1   Initial stages of stock market development in China

	Balance of shares outstanding	Value of shares traded on stock exchanges
1986	6.0	
1987	10.0	
1988	35.0	0.2
1989	41.6	2.3
1990	45.9	

Note: The unit for all data is RMB billion.

Sources:
1.   *ACFB 1991*, p. 87.
2.   Tam, 1991, p. 514.

in certain reform-orientated cities and the expansion of such experiments were sanctioned by the central government (Bowles and White, 1992, pp. 578, 579). The year 1984 was the first time an SOE was permitted to issue shares to the public in Beijing. In 1985 the issuing of shares by SOEs became more widespread to cities such as Chongqing, Shanghai, Nanjing and Chengdu (Tam, 1991, pp. 520, 521). During the mid to late 1980s the central government became increasingly concerned that share issues were having negative implications for macroeconomic stability, contributing to over-investment and inflationary pressures. For this reason, in 1987 the State Council temporarily banned SOEs from issuing shares to the public (Bowles and White, 1992, p. 581). The limited involvement of the central government in stock market development during the first stage is reflected in that there were no formal national regulations surrounding the issuance of shares until 1987. Even the regulations issued in 1987 only outlined the principles that were to govern the issuance of shares by enterprises. Specific regulations were left to local governments (Tam, 1991, p. 527).

Apart from the wavering support of the central government, the first stage of stock market development was also characterized by essentially only a primary market for shares, with very few shares being traded on organized exchanges (Table 6.1). There was no nationwide secondary market for share trading, although a number of small regional exchanges existed in Shanghai, Beijing, Shenyang and a few other provincial cities (Singh, 1990, p. 167). During this time very few shares were made available to individuals and the general public, a factor that would have contributed to the sluggish development of secondary markets. For example, even by year end 1991, Chen (1994, p. 3) reports that only 2 percent of stock issuing companies had their shares publicly traded. Furthermore, of that 2 percent, private individuals held only 14 percent of the total shares on offer.

Another characteristic of the first stage of stock market development was that the shares on offer were vastly different to those found in stock markets in most countries. For one, they often featured a guaranteed rate of return. Second, they frequently did not confer any ownership rights on the holder such as representation on the firm's management committee. Thus, in these respects the shares on offer were more akin to bonds than shares as tradition-ally defined (Tam, 1991, p. 518). Third, there were numerous types of shares issued, even for a single shareholding company (Chen, 1994, p. 7). State shares were created when an SOE was converted to a shareholding corporate structure. These shares were held and managed by a state asset management organization or an administrative unit authorized by a state asset management organization. Enterprise shares were created when enterprises reinvested part of their after-tax profits back into the firm. Enterprise shares were held by the enterprise itself and were not transferable directly to individuals or workers. Workers did, however, indirectly benefit in that profits made on enterprise shares were divided into an accumulation fund, a public welfare fund and bonuses distributed to staff and workers. Individual shares included any shares issued to an individual natural person. Citing sample survey evidence from twelve provinces and municipalities across China in 1988, Tam (1991, p. 519) shows that state shares accounted for 36.6 percent of the total shares issued, enterprise shares accounted for 43.3 percent and individual shares 20.1 percent.

There were two key factors that fueled the formation of stock markets during the first stage of development. First, shares were used as a means to overcome restrictions and deficiencies in other sectors of the economy such as the banking system. Tam (1991, p. 522) describes the development of stock markets during this time as 'the result of rational reactions by the country's economic agents, now operating more autonomously, to seek maxi-mum returns on their activities'. Shares were attractive to surplus agents seeking to achieve higher returns on their savings than could be achieved through deposits in financial intermediaries. Bowles and White (1992, p. 581) report that the annual rate of return on shares issued by collective enterprises in 1985–86 was as high as 20–40 percent. This compared with a one-year savings time-deposit rate in the state banking system of around 7 percent (*ACFB 1990*, p. 171). Share issues were also used frequently as a device to raise the level of wages and bonuses to workers in an attempt to avoid taxes and bank supervision over total remuneration. Issuing shares to workers for such purposes was particularly common with SOEs (Tam, 1991, pp. 518, 521). The second key factor driving stock market development was the rap-idly rising level of income and surplus in the economy, particularly in the household sector. For example, in 1978 the annual per-capita disposable income of urban residents stood at just RMB343.4. By 1990, this had jumped to RMB1510.2 (SSB, 1999, p. 317).

Stock market development in China largely stalled over the period 1989–91. This was the result of economic factors such as rising inflation and financial instability, along with political factors such as the Tiananmen Square incident. Bowles and White (1992, p. 579) report that while there were plans to implement a nationwide network of stock markets in the late 1980s, these were shelved in light of the above factors. Ma (1995, p. 163) shows that the number of shareholding companies in China actually fell during the period 1988 to 1991.

The year 1991 marked the beginning of the second stage of stock market development in China. The active promotion and guidance of stock market development by the central government has characterized this stage. The policies for practicing the shareholding system are outlined in 1992 regulations titled 'Trial Measures on the Shareholding System', which was issued jointly by several central government connected agencies including the State Economic Restructuring Committee, the State Planning Committee, the Ministry of Finance, the PBC and the State Council Production Office. These regulations define the central government's purposes for promoting stock market development. It states that the shareholding system is to be applied to an enterprise in order to enhance the efficiency of state assets, to facilitate the efficient allocation of social resources and to change the enterprise into an independent economic entity responsible for its own profits and losses by separating government ownership from enterprise management (Yao, 1998, p. 5). Thus, stock market development during this second stage of development has primarily been promoted by the central government as a means of facilitating the reform of SOEs.

The influence of the central government can be seen through several characteristics of China's stock markets during the second stage of development. For one, the central government was behind the institutional reform that occurred in the early 1990s. The central government established two stock exchange hubs, one in Shanghai and the other in Shenzhen. Regional securities trading centers (there were 27 as of March 1997) were linked up to these hubs. Thus, a nationwide system of share trading was established (Yao, 1998, p. 44). Second, the central government has exercised a strong influence over the listing process. Each year, the State Council decides on the number of firms that are to be converted to shareholding enterprises and the total amount of capital to be raised. This annual plan is then allocated to the various provincial governments taking into account geographical and industry needs. Provincial governments then call for applications and select firms for listing. Final approval for listing is then required by the China Securities Regulatory

Commission. As a result of this process, the firms selected for listing on China's stock markets closely reflect the preferences of the central government. For one, firms selected for listing are almost exclusively SOEs (*ACFB 1997*, p. 71; PBC, 1998, p. 55). Second, listed firms are from selected sectors of the economy. The 1992 regulations prohibit stock issuance from sectors pertaining to 'national security, national defense technology, rare metals mining, or any lines of business that calls for a state monopoly'. A 1996 circular further temporarily prohibited stock issuance from the financial industry and the real estate industry (Yao, 1998, p. 5). The majority of listed firms are from the industrial sector, in particular manufacturing (*ESMFB 2000*, p. 75). Third, stock market access has varied depending upon the size of the firm, with medium and large-scale operations receiving the bulk of representation. Song et al. (1998, p. 129) states that 78 percent of listed companies are amongst the 10 largest companies in their respective economic sectors. Fourthly, the government regulates the initial offering price of shares in the primary market (Yao, 1998, p. 7). Finally, the government decides upon the share structure of a listing company, with the primary objective in most cases being to ensure the dominance of state ownership. Yao (1998, p. 22) reports that according to a 1996 government report, 68 percent of the total share interests of listed companies were controlled by the state in the form of state shares or state-owned legal person shares. Trade in these shares was either banned or highly restricted. This left a maximum of 32 percent of shares available for trade in the secondary market amongst members of the Chinese public. The government also uses the share structure to control the extent to which foreign investors can buy equity stakes in China's listed companies. This is done by delineating individual shares into two categories, A and B shares. A shares are domestically listed shares that can be purchased only by Chinese citizens, whereas B shares are reserved solely for foreigners. In 2000, only 114 of China's 1088 listed companies had been permitted to offer B shares (SSB, 2001, p. 641).

The Extent of Stock Market Development

In the empirical literature, there are numerous measures that are used to gauge the extent of stock market development, relating to factors such as size, liquidity and volatility (Levine and Zervos, 1998). The logic behind including size as a measure of stock market development is obvious. The logic behind including liquidity is that as stock markets develop, liquidity should improve as impediments to the trading of shares such as poor infrastructure and high trading taxes decline. Volatility should fall as prudential frameworks are strengthened and information on listed firms is disseminated in a more complete and timely manner. Stock market size is typically measured by the market capitalization ratio (MC), which is the total value of outstanding shares (market capitalization), expressed as a percentage of GDP. The standard measure of liquidity is the turnover ratio (TR), which is equal to the total value of shares traded, expressed as a percentage of market capitalization. Volatility (VOL) in this chapter is measured simply by calculating the standard deviation of the monthly percentage changes in the Shanghai composite share price index. Table 6.2 tracks these measures over the period 1991–99. The data suggest that China's stock markets have undergone considerable development, which has been reflected through increased size and reduced volatility. There is no clear trend in liquidity.

Table 6.2   The development of national stock markets in China

	MC	TR	VOL
1991	0.5		
1992	3.9	65.0	
1993	10.2	103.9	26.3
1994	7.9	220.2	42.7
1995	5.9	126.5	11.9
1996	14.5	216.7	10.7
1997	23.5	175.3	8.6
1998	24.6	120.7	6.3
1999	32.3	118.3	11.1

Sources:
1.   PBC, various years.
2.   *ESMFB* various years.

The finding that China's stock markets have grown, however, does not necessarily imply that they have become an important financial structure within China, or that they have grown relatively quickly or slowly as compared to other developing countries. To shed light on these questions, a comparative analysis is needed. Table 6.3 compares the savings mobilized by the stock market with other domestic securities and domestic financial institutions in China. This is instructive because it shows that while China's stock markets may have grown rapidly in recent years, they remain a marginal source of savings mobilization.

Given that stock market development is at least partially dependent upon the level of economic development, it is also informative to place the development of China's stock markets in an international comparative perspective to determine if they have grown relatively quickly or slowly. One way this

Table 6.3   *Savings mobilized via stock markets, other domestic securities and financial institutions*

	Stock markets	Other domestic securities	Financial institutions
1991	5.0		4 066.4
1992	94.1		5 389.0
1993	233.0		6 159.0
1994	365.1	2 075.3	10 845.5
1995	56.0	1 727.0	13 209.7
1996	271.6	3 172.3	14 889.0
1997	735.8	4 098.5	13 819.1
1998	468.6	5 757.6	13 307.6
1999	576.4		13 081.0

Notes:
1. The unit for all data is RMB100 million.
2. The data for stock markets refer to the capital raised through A and B share issues on China's stock markets. The data for other domestic securities refer to the total value of issued securities such as government bonds, corporate bonds, etc. The data for financial institutions refer to the amount of new deposits in China's financial institutions. They are calculated as the change in outstanding year end balances.
3. A blank space signifies that data were unavailable.

Sources:
1. *SSB*, various years.
2. *ACFB 1997*, p. 161.
3. *CMS*, various issues.

can be done is by regressing a measure of stock market development against a measure of economic development for a large sample of countries to gauge an average relationship between stock market size and economic development. The measure of stock market development selected for this investigation is MC and the measure of economic development used is GNP per capita (GNPCAP). Thus, the estimated equation takes the form:

$$MC_t = \alpha_0 + \beta_1 GNPCAP_t + e_t \tag{6.1}$$

where α_0 and e_t are the intercept and error terms respectively. To estimate this equation, data for a sample of 100 countries were obtained for the year 1998. The source is *ESMFB 2000*. MC is calculated as market capitalization divided by GNP where both variables are measured in terms of $US. GNPCAP for all countries is converted to $US using purchasing power parity exchange

Table 6.4   Model results, dependent variable: MC

Coefficient	$\hat{\beta}_i$	$S_{\hat{\beta}_i}$ (p-value)
α_0	2.402	5.909 (0.407)
$GNPCAP_t$	0.004	0.001 (000)

$R^2 = 0.43$
$F_{(1, 98)} = 76.74$ (0.000)

rates. The estimated relationship returned by the simple OLS regression analysis is presented in Table 6.4.

As expected, MC displays a positive and highly statistically significant relationship with GNPCAP. China's actual GNPCAP can then be substituted into this estimated relationship in order to arrive at an expected MC based on China's level of economic development. According to this method, based on China's GNPCAP of $US3051 in 1998, the expected MC for China would be 14.57. This is less than China's actual MC of 24.6 and hence suggests that the development of China's stock markets is advanced relative to the stage of economic development. There are, however, some limitations with the above procedure. First, because MC is a function of stock prices, it can fluctuate considerably over a short time period. Thus, MC can only be looked up as a rough measure of stock market development (*ESMFB 2000*, p. 18). Second, the estimated expected MC is sensitive to the GNPCAP figure used. In the above example, the GNPCAP figure was an average value for all of China. GNPCAP, however, varies greatly across provinces. Given that China's stock markets are located in the more wealthy coastal regions of China, it could be argued that the usage of a national average is inappropriate. For example, in 1998 per capita GDP in Shanghai was RMB28 253 compared with a national average of RMB6 392 (SSB, 1999, pp. 55, 65). If this higher provincial figure were used the above finding may well be reversed and it could be concluded that the development of China's stock markets is quite low relative to the stage of economic development. This conclusion would seem to be more consistent with the finding of Table 6.3 that the importance of stock markets remain marginal relative to other financial institutions and markets, and the earlier discussion that highlighted considerable differences between China's stock markets and those found in more developed countries.

In summary, the development of stock markets in China is consistent with the predictions of theory; namely that both factors endogenous and exogenous to the process of economic development can be identified as driving their development. Nevertheless, despite government promotion and rapid growth in recent years, the structure of China's financial system remains heavily bank dominated, and therefore bears more in common with the financial systems of Japan and Germany, rather than the US and UK where the stock market plays a central role.

STOCK MARKETS AND ECONOMIC DEVELOPMENT: LITERATURE SURVEY

The theoretical and empirical literature concerning stock markets and economic development is vast and this section does not attempt to cover it in its entirety. Like financial institutions, the channels through which stock markets influence economic development are (a) the savings rate, (b) the quantity of investment and (c) the quality of investment (Singh, 1997, p. 774). On a microeconomic level, such channels can be discussed in terms of the impact on corporate finance and corporate governance. However, it is also important to consider on a macroeconomic level whether the overall level of savings has been affected. Otherwise, for example, it could be that the introduction and promotion of stock markets simply causes a substitution by savers towards holding shares instead of bank deposits, while the overall level of investment funds remains constant. This, of course, is not to say that such a substitution could not impact on economic development, such as in the case where financial institutions or stock markets allocate funds relatively more efficiently than the other.

Traditionally, an important debate in the literature has been whether a stock market-based financial system or a bank-based system impacts upon channels (a)–(c) more effectively. The corporate governance role of financial institutions and markets in particular is often discussed in terms of two distinct models (Mayer, 1994, p. 189). The first model is labeled the outsider, stock market based approach (OS) and is associated most notably with the US and the UK. Under the OS model, firm ownership is typically diffuse and individual shareholders are outsiders in the sense that they only have arm's length input into the firm's decision making through a board of directors. Corporate governance in this model is performed primarily through a market for corporate control. Therefore, the stock market plays a central role in corporate governance via the takeover mechanism. The second model is labeled the insider, bank-based model (IB) and is most typically associated with Germany and Japan. In the IB model, firm ownership is concentrated in the hands of a few key shareholders that rarely trade their shares. Corporate governance is exercised from within the firm by these insiders rather than through a market for corporate control. Banks, rather than stock markets, feature predominantly in this model. Their influence is through several channels, including being important suppliers of external finance, holders of firm equity and holding seats on the firm's management board (Corbett, 1994, p. 316). With respect to transitional economies, there is considerable debate as to whether such economies are best served by the OS or IB model (Popov, 1999, p. 1). On the one hand, the IB model seems the most natural choice because banks are already established and have a history of lending to firms (Aoki, 1995). Stock markets only exist in embryonic form in many transitional economies and hence cannot be expected to play a significant role in corporate financing and governance, at least in the short and medium term. Scholtens (2000, p. 535) also argues that stock markets require a much more elaborate legal system and prudential framework than banks to function effectively. On the other hand, it could be argued that there is little scope for the development of bank-led corporate governance because the SOBs that dominate the financial sector in transitional economies are not skilled in making decisions according to commercial principles (Rowstowsi, 1995).

Empirical studies examining the impact of stock markets on economic development have produced some important insights. Earlier studies based on international panel data returned differing results. For example, Atje and Jovanovic (1993), using a data set of 39 countries over the period 1980–88, found that a positive and statistically significant relationship existed between stock markets and economic growth. However, this result was later criticized by Harris (1997) on the basis of the methodology employed. Using an expanded data set and an alterative model specification, Harris (1997) concluded that the evidence suggesting that stock markets promote economic development was 'at best very weak'. More recent studies by Levine and Zervos (1998) and Khan and Senhadji (2000) have been particularly informative due to the utilization of nested models and more detailed model specifications that consider separately the channels through which financial institutions and markets impact upon economic development. The findings of these studies suggest that (a) stock markets and financial institutions are not necessarily competing in nature, but rather are complementary with both potentially positively impacting on economic development, and (b) the stock market has its greatest impact on economic development through its creation of liquidity. This finding acts as confirmation for earlier theories that postulated that the liquidity provided by stock markets raises the productivity of capital on an economy-wide level because it facilitates longer term, profitable investment (Demirguc-Kunt and Levine, 1996, p. 229).

Another important contribution of recent empirical studies has been to show that the impact stock markets have on economic development appears to display considerable diversity between individual countries. For example, evidence presented by Arestis and Demetriades (1997, pp. 785–790) concluded that the relationship between stock markets and economic development in the US was largely positive but insignificant in the case of Germany. Such findings should not be surprising. Okuda (1990, p. 240), for example, earlier noted that the causal link between financial factors and economic development is crucially dependent upon the nature and operation of financial institutions, markets and policies pursued by individual countries. Therefore, while the findings of studies using international panel data are informative, they also need to be complemented by individual country case studies. The following is a preliminary contribution to this endeavour in the case of China.

THE IMPACT OF STOCK MARKETS ON ECONOMIC DEVELOPMENT IN CHINA

Data constraints seriously impinge upon an empirical investigation into the impact of stock markets on China's economic development. Typically, only financial data such as stock prices and trading volumes are available, which goes a long way to explaining why the bulk of previous studies examining China's stock markets have been from a financial economics perspective rather than a development economics one. This research primarily makes use of a relatively comprehensive data set of China's listed companies published on-line at www.chinaweb.com. This site is produced by ChinaWeb Ltd, in association with contributors such as Homeway, a leading provider of financial services in China, and the *South China Morning Post*, Hong Kong's leading English language news provider. It makes available selected data on China's listed firms, with the information being sourced from the latest available company annual reports (1999 or 2000).

To consider the corporate financing contribution of stock markets, the ideal approach is to compare the relative importance of internal financing, external equity financing and external debt financing in explaining the growth of net corporate assets (Singh and Weiss, 1998, p. 610). Unfortunately, data limitations prevent such an analysis from being conducted here. To shed light on this issue, the equity/asset ratio for each company was first calculated. This data was available for 902 listed companies. The mean equity/asset ratio returned was 53.1 percent (median = 54.2). While this result does not shed light on the importance of equity capital relative to other financing sources, it does nonetheless indicate that equity financing in an absolute sense has been a significant source of finance for listed companies.

Considering the liability/asset ratio of listed companies is also useful in gauging the importance of equity financing. Liabilities of non-listed SOEs consist almost exclusively of bank loans and in recent years have reached extremely high levels. Indeed, one of the key objectives of listing SOEs is to reduce their dependence upon debt finance. There are two simple ways that can be used to test if equity financing has reduced dependence upon debt financing. First, looking at listed firms, one would expect to see a negative correlation between the equity/asset ratio and the liability/asset ratio. That is, those firms which have been permitted greater access to equity financing, should have been able to reduce their liability/asset ratio and their dependence on debt to a larger extent. Relevant data were available for 915 companies. The results confirm a strong negative correlation between these two series, with a correlation coefficient of −0.97.

Second, if equity financing has been significant, it could also be expected that listed firms (formerly SOEs) would have a lower liability/asset ratio than SOEs taken as a whole. For reasons of data availability, this study focuses solely on comparing listed firms from the industrial sector with state-owned industrial firms taken as a whole. Focusing on industrial firms is also warranted because the bulk of China's listed companies are from the industrial sector, with a minority coming from sectors such as real estate development, retailing, tourism, transport and finance. Aggregate data for all industrial SOEs in 1999 are available from SSB (2000, pp. 414–417), while data on listed companies are sourced from the on-line database acknowledged earlier. In order to make these data series as comparable as possible, two actions were first undertaken. First, listed firms from non-industrial sectors of the economy were removed from the calculations. Deciding whether to include or exclude a listed firm is not always a clear-cut matter given that several are conglomerates and undertake activities in numerous sectors of the economy. Therefore, as a rule, if industrial activities constituted the primary business activity of a listed firm, it was retained for the comparison. After this filtering process, 747 listed companies were retained. Second, it was also necessary to remove that component of industrial SOEs' assets that are used for non-industrial production. This is because non-listed industrial SOEs provide a variety of services to workers such as schools and hospitals to name a few. However, in the process of listing, these assets are removed the from firm's books. The percentage of industrial SOEs' assets not used for industrial production has been placed at around 18 percent by Jefferson et al. (1996, p. 176). However, Xu and Wang (1997, p. 11) state that such non-productive assets typically account for between 25–50 percent of the to-be-listed firm's total assets. A figure of 25 percent has been used for this study. After these steps have been undertaken, the estimated average liability/asset ratio of listed industrial firms was 43.96 percent. The figure for all industrial SOEs meanwhile was 82 percent. Thus, this result is supportive of the view that external equity financing has been a significant source of funding for listed firms and useful in terms of reducing their liability/asset ratio.

The corporate financing impact of the stock market should nevertheless not be exaggerated. It has been an insignificant source of financing for non-state-owned firms, with Gregory and Tenev (2001) stating that in 1999 only 1 percent of listed firms were non-state firms. PBC (1999, pp. 57–60) also shows that stock issuances, in both local and foreign currencies, accounted for only 1.3 percent of total corporate financing in 1995, 3.2 percent in 1996, 8.7 percent in 1997 and 6.0 percent in 1998. This compared with 10.7 percent, 14.0 percent, 14.3 percent and 11.4 percent for bonds and commercial papers, and 88.0 percent, 82.8 percent, 77.0 percent and 82.6 percent for financial institution lending.

To gauge the corporate governance effects of China's stock markets, the ratio of net profits to assets was calculated for each listed company. This data was available for 925 listed companies. Unfortunately, measures directly considering economic efficiency such as the productivity of capital could not be calculated due to the necessary data being unavailable. Nevertheless, calculating profitability is still relevant because one of the stated corporate governance objectives in transforming SOEs into listed companies is to make them more responsible for their own profits and losses. The average ratio of net profits/assets was just 3.60 percent (median = 4.08). In addition, 9.19 percent of all companies had a net profit/asset ratio of less than 0. To put the profitability of listed firms in a comparative perspective, the net profit/asset ratio for all industrial SOEs (after non-productive assets have been removed) was 1.65 percent, 4.33 percent for collective firms, 3.78 percent for all shareholding companies (many shareholding companies are not listed on public exchanges), 3.56 percent foreign funded firms and 2.99 percent for firms funded from sources based in Hong Kong, Macao or Taiwan (SSB, 2000, pp. 414–417). Thus, in this context, the corporate governance impact of stock market appears comparable with that achieved by other industrial firms featuring non-state ownership. There is, however, one factor that makes the comparative financial performance of listed firms alarming and raises concerns about the corporate governance impact of the stock market. Firms selected for listing on China's stock exchanges are not drawn in a random manner. As noted by Yao (1998, p. 6), it is a prerequisite condition for a firm to attain a stock market listing that it must have been profitable for the previous three years. Based on a Ministry of Finance survey of 40 000 state-owned industrial enterprises, PBC (1999, p. 58) notes that the financial conditions in nearly half of these enterprises fell short of the regulatory requirement for listing. As a result, Xu and Wang (1997, p. 3) make the point that it is important to realize that 'Publicly-listed companies, however, represent only a small subset of China's enterprises – a clean and perhaps better performed group of enterprises which were chosen to be listed on the two stock exchanges'. Thus, the fact that the data indicate that roughly 10 percent of listed companies now have a negative net profit/asset ratio, despite the short history of China's stock markets, suggests some serious corporate governance problems exist. Regulatory guidelines also specify that for a listed company to be able to raise additional funds through the stock market, they must achieve a rate of return on net assets of at least 10 percent. Thus, at present many listed firms are unable to again use the stock market as a source of external financing (PBC, 1999, p. 59). The poor financial performance of listed firms is also highlighted by Heytens and Karacadag (2001), who found evidence of declining rates of profitability, vulnerability to even modest interest rates and demand shocks and estimated NPLs in the vicinity of 20–30 percent. This financial picture is backed by a recent study into the productivity growth of industrial firms of different ownership types. During the period 1993–96, Jefferson et al. (2000) found that the TFP growth performance of shareholding firms (listed and non-listed) ranked last when compared with state-owned firms, collectively-owned firms, 'other' domestic enterprises and foreign invested firms.

One corporate governance problem postulated by Tam (1999, p. 88) is that while the Chinese authorities have tried to impose a legal and regulatory framework borrowed from the US model of corporate governance, present conditions in China's stock markets are more akin to countries such as Germany and Japan. In particular, in contrast to the diffuse ownership of listed companies in the US, shareholding in China's listed companies remains highly concentrated. Based on the annual reports of China's listed companies in 1995, Xu and Wang (1997, p. 49) showed that the percentage of outstanding shares owned by the five largest shareholders averaged 58.1 percent. This compared with 25.4 percent in the US, 33.1 percent in Japan and 41.5 percent in Germany. The data set available for this research can be used to update Xu and Wang's data to see if any change in ownership concentration has occurred. Ownership concentration data were available for 910 listed companies. The results showed that the ownership share of the top five shareholders has remained practically unchanged over the past five years with a mean value of 58.39 percent (median = 59.81). The extremely small ownership share of minority shareholders is also clearly evidenced by the data. For example, expanding the calculation to the ownership concentration share of the top 10 shareholders only slightly increases the mean value to 60.99 (median = 62.55). The ownership share of the single largest shareholder averaged 44.22 percent (median = 43.46). In 369 companies, or 40.55 percent of the listed companies for which data were available, the ownership share of the largest shareholder was equal to or greater than 50 percent.

However, as illustrated by the experiences of countries such as Germany and Japan, higher ownership concentration per se need not result in a failure of corporate governance. The key problem in the case of China's stock markets is that the high ownership concentration actually reflects the continuing dominance of state ownership in many listed companies. This is a point of departure from the German and Japanese model of corporate governance. For example, OECD (1995, p. 17) showed that in 1993 public authorities only owned 1 percent of outstanding corporate equity in Japan and 4 percent in the case of Germany. Dominant state ownership means that the traditional incentive problems facing SOEs have not changed. As long as the state continues to be the primary shareholder, the corporate governance impact of 'insiders' on the firm's performance will be suboptimal. Furthermore, because shares controlled by the state cannot be legally traded, the market for corporate control where 'outsiders' exercise governance is compromised. To estimate the degree to which this has occurred, the proportion of tradable shares to total outstanding shares was calculated. This data was available for 913 companies. The average ratio of tradable shares to total outstanding shares was just 38.53 percent (median = 36.70). In only 8.32 percent of companies was the ratio greater than 50 percent. Thus, a market for corporate control is nonexistent for the overwhelming majority of listed companies and it can be concluded that managers face only a limited threat of punishment for poor decision making from either 'insiders' or 'outsiders'. It should also be noted that the influence of the state runs ever deeper than their dominant ownership position. For example, Xu and Wang (1999, pp. 82, 83) showed that the state's representation on the board of directors of many listed companies far outweighed that which could be justified even on the basis of their sizeable ownership stake.

The ideal approach to empirically investigating the impact of stock markets on macroeconomic channels to growth such as the rate of savings is to regress the various determinants of savings including stock market parameters, against the rate of savings (Bonser-Neal and Dewenter, 1999). Unfortunately, this would not be a meaningful approach in the case of China given that only annual data since 1991 are available for many required variables. However, what is useful is to recall the findings of Table 6.3, which showed that the savings mobilization performance of China's stock market lags behind other domestic securities markets and far behind that of financial institutions. Therefore, any impact stock markets may have had on aggregate savings must have been small.

This conclusion also applies to the impact of stock markets on the allocative efficiency of capital at a macroeconomic level. Bearing this in mind, the allocative efficiency effects of stock markets can be considered in more depth by evaluating the informational efficiency and fundamental valuation efficiency of the stock pricing mechanism. Testing for the informational efficiency of stock prices revolves around examining whether stock prices behave in a manner implied by the Efficient Market Hypothesis (EMH). The EMH contends that if stock prices are efficient in an informational sense, they will rapidly adjust to new information and that current prices will fully absorb and reflect all available information (Mookerjee and Yu, 1999). Empirical testing of the EMH involves testing whether current stock prices and returns can be predicted on the basis of past values. If stock prices are efficient then these variables should display a random walk process. Otherwise, the stock pricing mechanism can be considered inefficient because investors can theoretically achieve profits simply by utilizing available information such as past prices. Numerous empirical studies on the behavior of stock prices in China have concluded that they do not follow a random walk process (Song et al., 1998; Su and Fleisher, 1998; Mookerjee and Yu, 1999). Testing whether stock prices accurately reflect the economic fundamentals underlying a firm is conceptually more difficult. However, the degree of stock price volatility can serve as a useful guide. For example, if stock prices are driven by speculative motives and herding behavior, then they will be highly volatile and represent inefficient signals for capital flows in the economy (Singh, 1997, p. 774). For much of their short history, the stock markets in Shanghai and Shenzhen have been highly volatile and numerous instances of price bubbles can be easily cited. In one instance, Shanghai's composite price index doubled in a single day (Su and Fleisher, 1998, p. 250). Xu and Wang (1999, p. 95) also note that the speculative nature of shareholding in China amongst individual investors is apparent by the fact that the average period for which they held shares was just 1–2 months. This compared with 18 months in the US. Many researchers and observers, including the PBC, have expressed the view that stock prices are excessively volatile in the sense that they often reflect speculative activities rather than the economic fundamentals of listed firms (PBC, 1994 p. 54; Spencer, 1995, p. 29; Mookerjee and Yu, 1999). The fact that shares controlled by the state cannot be traded worsens the degree of share price volatility. When only a small proportion of a company's total shares are available for trading, share prices cannot reflect the market's view of the fundamental value of a listed firm (Spencer, 1995, p. 30; Yao, 1998, p. 22). However, it should be noted that this volatility does appear to have declined in the most recent years. For example, Table 6.2 showed that the standard deviation in the Shanghai composite share price index (based on monthly observations) fell from a high of 42.7 in 1994 to 11.1 in 1999.

To gauge the extent of volatility in China's stock markets it is also informative to compare the Chinese experience with other large developing and/or transitional countries. Table 6.5 compares stock market volatility in China with Brazil, India, Hungary and Poland. These data lend support to the view that while China's stock markets were initially relatively volatile, this situation has diminished in recent years.

Table 6.5   Stock market volatility in China: a comparative perspective

	China	Brazil	India	Hungary	Poland
1993	26.2	11.1	8.7	8.2	31.1
1994	42.7	31.1	8.5	18.8	24.0
1995	11.9	12.3	5.5	8.0	14.9
1996	10.7	6.0	8.3	11.6	11.9
1997	8.6	12.2	7.1	11.7	7.5
1998	6.3	17.0	8.2	15.3	12.5
1999	11.1	10.3	9.0	8.8	8.9

Note: As in Table 6.2, volatility is measured by calculating the standard deviation of the monthly percentage changes in the respective country's share price indices.

Source: *ESMFB*, various years.

CONCLUSION

Taken as a whole, the findings of the previous section indicate that the impact of the stock market on China's economic development has been limited. In particular, the data highlighted serious concerns over the corporate governance impact of the stock market on reforming SOEs. This is an important finding because it implies that the continual usage and promotion of the stock market almost solely for the purpose of SOE reform is a deficient policy choice, at least as long as the commitment to majority state ownership of listed companies is maintained. It also implies that the central government will have to look to alternative corporate governance strategies in their bid to improve the performance of SOEs and promote their reform.

The one area where the stock market did appear to be quite successful was in raising funds for the modernization and restructuring of listing SOEs. However, the wider impact of the stock market as a channel for raising funds for investment should not be exaggerated. First, on a microeconomic level, because nearly all listed firms are ex-SOEs, the stock market has been an insignificant source of external financing for non-state-owned firms. Second, on a macroeconomic level, the total amount of funds raised on the stock market has been insignificant relative to the aggregate amount of savings in China.

Finally, the evidence suggested that the stock market has not yet significantly improved the efficiency with which capital is allocated in the economy. In large part this was due to the fact that stock markets only allocate a small percentage of total savings in China. Evidence from previous studies also point to the fact that the efficiency of the stock pricing mechanism as a signal for capital flows has often been lacking. Also, given that the impact of the stock market on the corporate governance of listed companies was dubious, the most efficient firms were not necessarily utilizing the funds raised.

7. External financial liberalization in China

INTRODUCTION

The previous chapters have dealt almost exclusively with issues relating to domestic financial reform in China. However, financial reform also has an external element. External financial liberalization (EFL), the topic of this chapter, can be defined as the removal of barriers to the free flow of capital between countries (Eichengreen et al., 1998, p. 2). At least in theory, economists have traditionally looked upon EFL as a means to promote economic development and maximize national wealth (Makin, 1994, p. 93). This is for two primary reasons. First, access to foreign capital can promote domestic growth by allowing a country to invest more than its saves, or import more than it exports. Second, it can increase the efficiency of investment by allowing funds to reach those projects that offer the highest rate of expected return on an international scale.

However, the experience of numerous developing countries has shown that these benefits do not come automatically. As once again evidenced by the Asian crisis in 1997, far from being growth inducing, EFL has frequently coincided with an unsustainable increase in foreign debt and domestic consumption, a rash of unproductive investment and sharp fluctuations in exchange rates, equity indices and asset prices (Diaz-Alenjandro, 1985; McKinnon and Pill, 1996). A modeling exercise conducted by McKibbin and Tang (2000) sought to gauge the consequences of China undertaking rapid EFL. The model's predictions depended crucially on the assumptions made regarding investor confidence. When EFL coincided with confidence in the Chinese economy, large capital inflows resulted and investment and real GDP were left permanently higher. However, even in this optimistic scenario, the real and nominal exchange rate appreciated close to 50 percent, crowding out net exports and leading to a deterioration in the current account position of nearly 4 percent. The impact on the exchange rate of overly exuberant investors following EFL in successful developing economies has already been discussed at length by McKinnon (1993). A large increase in the real exchange rate can in itself trigger a reversal of confidence as the current account position worsens and the sustainability of economic growth begins to be questioned. In the alternative scenario where EFL was followed by a loss of confidence in Chinese financial reforms, the predicted capital outflow was severe, causing consumption and investment to be below the level that would have been achieved if no EFL had been undertaken. In light of these potential dangers, calls for an acceleration of EFL in China as a means to promote economic development must be evaluated carefully.

The topic of EFL in China is only scantily covered in the existing literature. Therefore, this chapter has two primary objectives. First, it aims to contribute to the understanding of EFL in China to date. Second, it seeks to evaluate whether China can look upon an accelerated program of EFL as a development promoting strategy in its current state. The chapter begins by describing the nature of EFL that has occurred in China during the reform period. The extent to which EFL has occurred is then considered by examining the extent to which the actual exchange rate has deviated from its equilibrium value and the extent to which controls over capital account transactions are used. An interesting observation to flow from this discussion is that China has not been a large net capital importer. This is a surprising observation given that economic theory suggests it should have been in light of a low capital/labor ratio. It is considered whether the slow pace of EFL, restricting the extent to which foreign capital flows have been able to enter China, has been a contributing factor to this outcome. The theoretical literature is then reviewed in order to determine the prerequisite conditions necessary for EFL to promote economic development. Finally, China's current state of affairs is evaluated in light of the theory.

THE NATURE OF EXTERNAL FINANCIAL LIBERALIZATION

Official statistics indicate that foreign capital inflows have been far more significant than Chinese capital outflows abroad. The most significant foreign capital inflows have come in the form of foreign direct investment (FDI). By the mid-1990s, China was the recipient of more FDI than any other developing country (Lardy, 1995, p. 1065). Table 7.1, column 2, shows that the volume of FDI in China has been on a rising trend, peaking at 6.22 percent of GDP in 1994. Since 1994, this ratio has fallen slightly, initially most likely the result of macroeconomic instability in the form of double-digit inflation, and more recently the result of slowing economic growth. It should also be noted that the official FDI figures are likely to be overestimated. This is because a significant proportion of FDI is actually round-trip capital of Chinese origin. That is, primarily in an effort to take advantage of preferential tax and other incentives afforded to FDI, some

Table 7.1   Foreign direct investment in China

	Total		Controlling Body	
	($US million)	(% GDP)	Region (%)	Ministry (%)
1982	429.9	0.15		
1983	635.2	0.21		
1984	1 257.6	0.41		
1985	1 658.5	0.54		
1986	1 874.9	0.63	73.2	26.8
1987	2 313.5	0.72	62.7	37.3
1988	3 193.7	0.80	82.0	18.0
1989	3 392.6	0.76	90.1	9.9
1990	3 487.1	0.89	90.9	9.1
1991	4 366.3	1.07	94.5	5.5
1992	10 007.5	2.07	97.4	2.6
1993	27 515.0	4.58	98.3	1.7
1994	33 766.5	6.22	98.0	2.0
1995	37 520.5	5.36	98.4	1.6
1996	41 725.5	5.11	99.4	0.6
1997	45 257.0	5.04	99.2	0.8
1998	45 462.8	4.74	99.6	0.4
1999	40 319.0	4.07	99.0	0.6
2000	40 715.0	3.77	99.1	0.9

Notes:
1. Official statistics classify China's usage of foreign capital inflows according to the value of contracts signed during a given year and by the amount actually utilized during a given year. All data in this chapter refer to the amount actually utilized unless stated otherwise.
2. GDP figures in this chapter have been converted to $US using official exchange rates.
3. A blank space signifies that data was unavailable.

Sources:
1. *ACFERT* various years.
2. SSB, various years.

Chinese firms have been able to move funds abroad and then bring it back under the guise of foreign investment. Due to the illegal nature of such activities and a scarcity of data, the volume of round-trip capital can only be speculated. Lardy (1995, p. 1067) reports that the World Bank in 1992 guessed that round-trip capital might comprise as much as 25 percent of gross investment inflows into China. The bulk of these funds are recycled through Hong Kong. It has been reported that roughly two-thirds of the 'foreign capital' invested in China from Hong Kong is in fact of mainland origin (*Hua Sheng Bao*, 23 August, 1999).

Several aspects of FDI liberalization can be noted. First, as shown in Table 7.1, columns 4 and 5, the decision making powers with respect to the screening and approval of FDI have increasingly been delegated away from the central authorities towards lower levels of government, particularly those located in coastal regions (Kueh, 1992, p. 646). For example, in 1984 the cities of Tianjin and Shanghai were granted the power to autonomously approve productive FDIs up to the value of $US30 million. Dalian and Guangzhou were given a $US10 million limit and other cities a $US5 million limit (*ACFERT 1985*, p. 405). These limits effectively transferred most of the FDI decision making power to the provinces given that the average size of FDIs (by contracted value) at this time was only $US1.33 million (*ACFERT 1985*, p. 1066). In a bid to further decentralize the screening and approval process the central government further tripled the limits for some cities in 1996 (*ACFERT 1997/8*, p. 153). A second aspect of FDI liberalization is that the Chinese authorities have relaxed ownership restrictions with respect to FDI inflows. Initially, most FDI entering China was confined to the form of joint venture enterprises. For example, during the period 1979–83, wholly owned foreign enterprises accounted for only 3 percent of total FDI inflows. By 1997, this share had grown to 36 percent (*ACFERT*, various years). Third, FDIs have been permitted increased managerial autonomy over time. Chai (1998, p. 156) states that an FDI's authority was initially severely circumscribed with respect to input, output, pricing, and financial decisions. Fourthly, early on in the reform period the Chinese authorities began to use various positive incentives to attract FDI. A common incentive was offering concessions on customs duties, industrial and commercial taxes, income tax and taxes on profit remittances (*ACFERT 1985*, p. 404). They also included reduced fees for land use, labor services, and other public utilities (Chai, 1998, p. 157). While these incentives were initially confined to FDIs located in special economic zones (SEZs), over time they became more widely available, particularly to those cities and provinces located in the coastal regions (Lardy, 1995, p. 1067; Chai, 1998, p. 158). Finally, controls over the economic sectors in which FDI can be conducted have been relaxed. For example, in its bid to enter the World Trade Organization (WTO), China has begun to open up its formerly closed services sectors, such as banking, retailing and telecommunications, as well as major infrastructure activities for foreign investment (Chai, 1998, p. 159).

The next most important type of foreign capital inflow has come in the form of foreign loans. Table 7.2, column 2, shows the volume of foreign loan inflows. It shows that while foreign loans dominated foreign capital inflows during the 1980s, they fell significantly behind FDI inflows during the 1990s.

Table 7.2   Foreign loans in China

	Total		Controlling body		Source			
	($US million)	(% GDP)	Region (%)	Ministry (%)	FG (%)	IFI (%)	CL (%)	EC (%)
1982	1 783.1	0.64						
1983	1 064.7	0.35	7.4	92.6				
1984	1 161.5	0.38	10.7	89.3	62.2	15.8	10.5	11.5
1985	1 743.6	0.57	11.2	88.8	27.9	34.7	30.2	7.3
1986	3 855.7	1.30	20.6	79.4	21.8	34.8	38.8	4.6
1987	4 565.6	1.42	24.6	75.4	17.5	15.7	56.5	10.4
1988	5 625.1	1.40	37.9	62.1	21.0	20.0	43.3	15.8
1989	6 144.6	1.37	38.4	61.6	35.0	17.6	36.9	10.4
1990	6 531.6	1.68	31.5	68.5	38.6	16.3	31.3	13.8
1991	6 779.1	1.67	33.6	66.4	26.7	20.1	36.0	17.1
1992	6 640.0	1.37	25.9	74.1	38.7	19.7	26.8	14.9
1993	9 800.7	1.63	25.8	74.2	31.0	23.1	33.4	12.5
1994	7 913.0	1.46	25.8	74.2	30.3	18.5	23.5	27.7
1995	9 544.0	1.36	24.3	75.7	29.1	28.4	14.6	28.0
1996	9 270.0	1.13	50.2	49.8	37.2	23.3	16.1	14.3
1997	9 614.0	1.07	10.7	89.3	37.7	17.0	31.9	13.4
1998	10 000.0	1.04			29.0	30.0	22.6	18.4
1999	9 412.0	0.95			35.2	27.7	26.2	10.9

Notes:
1. FG: Foreign governments; IFI: International Financial Institutions; CL: Commercial loans; EC: Export credit.
2. Official statistics list foreign funds raised through bonds and shares under the category of foreign loans. This is not conventional and hence when the total volume of foreign loans is presented in column 2, the value of these funds has been subtracted from the official total where possible. *ACFERT 1984* (p. 1095) provides only a total value for external loans in 1982 and 1983. Therefore, the data in column 2 for 1982 and 1983 are inclusive of bonds and shares. The volume of funds raised through bonds and shares during these years is likely to have been very small. The percentages given in columns 4 and 5 are calculated using the official total (that is, including bonds and shares) because the funds raised through bonds and shares are not separately disaggregated according to the controlling body. The percentages given in columns 6–9 are calculated according to the total given in column 2 (that is, exclusive of bonds and shares).

Sources:
1. *ACFERT*, various years.
2. SSB, various years.
3. SSO, 1990, pp. 552–553.

Table 7.2, columns 4 and 5 shows that while there is some evidence of decentralization in the control of foreign loans, it has been far less than that which has occurred with respect to FDI. It has also fluctuated somewhat as opposed to trending in one particular direction. Foreign borrowing in China is classified either as 'plan' or 'non-plan' borrowing (IMF, *AREAER 1998*, p. 115). Plan borrowing includes (1) borrowing by the government sector from foreign governments and international financial institutions; (2) external borrowing by Chinese financial institutions; (3) external borrowing by authorized Chinese enterprises; and (4) short-term trade credits over three months. Non-plan borrowing includes (1) borrowing by foreign funded enterprises; and (2) borrowing from branches of foreign banks or jointly invested banks operating in China. Within these categories, the State Planning Commission is responsible for coordinating foreign borrowing for projects included in the annual and five-year plans. Project executing agencies (such as the Ministry of Finance, provincial governments and so on) propose projects to the State Planning Commission. The State Planning Commission reviews these projects and then recommends to the State Council the overall number of projects and the associated financing.

Loans from foreign governments and international financial institutions require the clearance of the State Planning Commission and the approval of the State Council. Loans from the World Bank are the responsibility of the Ministry of Finance, those from the International Monetary Fund and the Asian Development Bank are the responsibility of the PBC, and those from foreign governments are the responsibility of the Ministry of Foreign Trade and Economic Cooperation. All medium and long-term commercial borrowing abroad under the plan requires the approval from the State Administration of Foreign Exchange (SAFE) and must be conducted through authorized Chinese financial institutions. Borrowing quotas are allocated under the annual plan. The SAFE permits institutions responsible for undertaking commercial borrowing to contract short-term loans up to specified limits without prior approval.

Some decentralization in the control over foreign commercial loans has occurred with regulations issued in 1991 that authorized the local branches of the SAFE and PBC to be responsible for the actual examination, approval, supervision and administration of such loans (*ACFERT 1992/3*, p. 202). As the control of foreign commercial loans became more decentralized, compliance with central government requirements fell. For example, despite the central government requirement that all foreign loans be registered, even SAFE has acknowledged that such regulations have been frequently violated (*ACFERT 1992/93*, p. 202). The evidence suggests that such circumvention of central controls has meant that China's usage of foreign commercial loans is far greater than that indicated by official statistics. Table 7.3 considers the extent of unregistered foreign commercial loans by comparing the official Chinese data with World Bank data. World Bank data differ from Chinese data primarily in that they supplement loan data reported by debtors with those reported by creditors through organizations such as the Bank for Inter-

Table 7.3　　The value and maturity of foreign commercial loans

	Official Chinese data	World Bank data	BIS data on short-term claims
1986	1 495	1 782	
1987	2 580	4 605	
1988	2 435	4 470	
1989	2 269	2 017	
1990	2 044	3 247	
1991	2 443	2 623	
1992	1 778	5 062	
1993	3 271	5 624	
1994	1 857	2 380	44.0
1995	1 395	4 977	47.6
1996	1 494	4 915	48.9
1997	3 069	5 889	53.4
1998	2 260	1 537	53.7
1999	2 465	2 086	40.6
2000			33.1

Note:　　BIS data on short-term claims is available only since 1994.

Sources:
1.　*ACFERT* various years.
2.　SSB, various years.
3.　World Bank, *GDF* various years.
4.　BIS, *Consolidated International Banking Statistics*, various editions.

national Settlements (BIS). Therefore, even if a loan contract was not officially registered in China, it would be picked up by the World Bank data when the crediting institution reported to the BIS. Table 7.3, column 2 presents the official Chinese data on the amount of foreign commercial loans utilized. Column 3 presents World Bank data on the value of long-term loan disbursements made to China by foreign commercial banks. Disbursements are defined as the drawing on loan commitments in a given year. By comparing columns 2 and 3 it can be seen that apart from 1989 and 1998–99, the World Bank data are consistently higher than the official Chinese data. The year 1989 represented a temporary recentralization in the control of foreign loans as the central government became concerned that excessive credit creation had contributed to the emergence of double-digit inflation. The year 1998 also represented a period of recentralization in response to the Asian financial crisis.

It should also be noted that because the World Bank data only relate to long-term lending (maturity ≥ 1 year), they can be regarded as minimum values. While data on the volume of short-term commercial lending are scarce, it has been reported that many of China's TICs borrowed funds from abroad on short-term maturities (van Kemenade, 1999, p. 171). This assertion seems to be supported by BIS consolidated international banking data. Table 7.3, column 4 shows that BIS reporting banks recently placed their short-term claims on China (maturity ≤ 1 year) at 33 percent of total consolidated claims, down from over 50 percent during 1997, the year of the Asian financial crisis.

Another aspect of foreign loan liberalization is that foreign commercial banks have been increasingly permitted to conduct operations directly in China. Initially, the operations of foreign banks were confined to the status of representative offices, which meant that they could not undertake activities directly related to generating a profit. They were also geographically confined to Beijing and the SEZs (*ACFB 1992*, p. 235). Over time, these constraints have been gradually relaxed. First, geographical restrictions over where foreign banks could set up an operational office were gradually relaxed and in 1999 they were eliminated entirely (PBC, 2000, p. 39). Second, 1987 regulations allowed foreign banks to begin increasing their business scope, enabling them to engage in profit-making activities such as loans, deposits, portfolio investment and guarantees (*ACFB 1992*, p. 240). However, their customer base was initially restricted to servicing foreign enterprises operating in China through foreign currency transactions, while the servicing of Chinese enterprises and individuals through local RMB transactions remained prohibited (*ACFB 1993*, p. 29). This restriction has also been gradually reduced over time. In December 1996, four foreign banks located in the Pudong district of Shanghai were permitted to engage in limited RMB business (*ACFB 1996*, p. 50). By year end 1999, the total assets of foreign banks in China had reached US$31 787 million, accounting for 1.53 percent of the total financial assets in China. Their foreign exchange loans totaled US$21 831 million, accounting for 12.81 percent of the foreign exchange loans in China, while their holdings of foreign exchange deposits remained relatively small at US$5198 million. At the same time their RMB assets stood at RMB11.2 billion, loans at RMB6.7 billion and deposits at RMB5.4 billion (PBC, 2000, p. 39). Thus, the foreign banks' share of the RMB loan and deposit markets continued to be miniscule, representing only 0.07 percent and 0.05 percent respectively. By year end 2001, the number of foreign financial institutions permitted to engage in RMB transactions had grown to 31 and their assets were RMB45 billion, with loans of over RMB39 billion (*China Daily*, 21 February 2002).

The least important type of foreign capital inflow into China has been in the form of portfolio investment (bonds and shares). The total amount of

Financial reform and economic development in China

Table 7.4   Foreign portfolio investment in China

	Total		Bonds	Shares
	($US million)	(% GDP)	($US million)	($US million)
1984	124.2	0.04	124.2	
1985	762.4	0.25	762.4	
1986	1 158.9	0.39	1 158.9	
1987	1 239.4	0.39	1 239.4	
1988	861.6	0.21	861.6	
1989	141.1	0.03	141.1	
1990	3.0	0.00	3.0	
1991	108.5	0.03		
1992	1 270.7	0.26		
1993	1 388.1	0.23		
1994	1 354.0	0.25		
1995	783.0	0.11		
1996	3 399.0	0.42		
1997	8 064.0	0.90	2 407.0	5 657.0
1998	1 622.3	0.17	1 000.0	622.3
1999	1 410.0	0.14	800.0	610.0

Notes:
1. Columns 4 and 5 show the relative importance of bonds and shares. Official statistics do not disaggregate the total value presented in column 2 until 1997. However, given that share purchases by foreigners were not permitted until 1991, all foreign funds raised must have been through bond issues.
2. A blank space signifies that data was unavailable.

Sources:
1. *ACFERT* various years.
2. SSB, various years.

foreign funds utilized through bond and share issues is presented in Table 7.4, column 2. The relative importance of each source is given in columns 4 and 5. Bonds clearly have a longer history in China and have been the most important type of foreign portfolio investment. However, the figures for 1997–98 do indicate that share issues have come to rival bonds in the most recent years.

The control over the issuance of bonds abroad has remained under the control of the central authorities. The headquarters of the PBC and the SAFE are responsible for the examination and approval of all bond issues abroad (*ACFB 1991*, p. 208; *1998*, p. 61). The overwhelming majority of domestic institutions that have been permitted to issue bonds abroad are connected to the central government, such as the Ministry of Finance and the Bank of China. Only a handful of regional institutions, such as selected TICs and large enterprises, have been granted permission to issue bonds abroad (*ACFB 1998*, p. 156). As was noted in Chapter 6, the control over the issuance of shares has also remained firmly in the hands of the central government.

One aspect of foreign portfolio investment liberalization is that there have been an increasing number of Chinese assets available for foreign purchase. Prior to 1991, the only assets available were bonds. In 1992, foreign portfolio equity investment was made possible through the establishment of B shares. In 1993, a number of Chinese companies were also given permission to list on overseas stock exchanges such as Hong Kong (H shares) and New York (N shares). In terms of capital raised, Table 7.5 shows that these overseas listings have been far more important in terms of raised capital than domestically listed B shares. Some large SOEs have also been able to raise large quantities of funds on the Hong Kong stock exchange by buying up small and/or inactive Hong Kong registered companies, moving assets into that company, and then selling shares on the Hong Kong stock exchange (so-called Red Chips). In 1997, overseas registered Chinese entities raised $US5.9 billion through issuing shares and convertible bonds in Hong Kong alone (*ACFB 1998*, p. 65).

Considering the nature of liberalization with respect to Chinese investment abroad is made difficult by data availability. As a result, Table 7.6 simply presents official balance of payments statistics. Column 2 shows the flow

Table 7.5   Domestic and overseas share listings: raised capital

	B shares	H shares/N shares
1992	4 409	
1993	3 813	6 093
1994	3 827	18 873
1995	3 335	3 146
1996	4 718	8 356
1997	8 076	36 000
1998	2 555	3 795
1999	379	4 717
2000	1 399	56 221

Note: The unit for all data is $US million.

Source: SSB, 2001, p. 642

Table 7.6　China's investment abroad

	FDIA		ΔPIAA		ΔLAA	
	($US million)	(% GDP)	($US million)	(% GDP)	($US million)	(% GDP)
1982	44	0.02	531	0.19		
1983	93	0.03	356	0.12		
1984	134	0.04	540	0.17		
1985	629	0.21	51	0.02	807	0.26
1986	450	0.15	40	0.01	406	0.14
1987	645	0.20	140	0.04	−151	0.05
1988	850	0.21	340	0.08	729	0.18
1989	780	0.17	320	0.07	121	0.03
1990	830	0.21	241	0.06	116	0.03
1991	913	0.22	330	0.08	48	0.01
1992	4 000	0.83	450	0.09	3 351	0.69
1993	4 400	0.73	597	0.10	1 741	0.29
1994	2 000	0.37	380	0.07	1 136	0.21
1995	2 000	0.29	−79	0.01	367	0.05
1996	2 114	0.26	628	0.08	1 102	0.13
1997	2 563	0.29	899	0.10	2 155	0.24
1998	2 634	0.27	3 830	0.40	1 411	0.15
1999	1 775	0.18	10 535	0.06	3 436	0.35

Note:　A blank space indicates that data was either unavailable or insignificant.

Source:　IMF, *BOPS*, various years.

amount of Chinese foreign direct investment abroad (FDIA), column 4 shows the change in Chinese holdings of portfolio investment assets abroad (ΔPIAA), and column 6 shows the change in Chinese holdings of loan assets abroad (ΔLAA).

The official data suggest that the most important type of Chinese investment abroad has been FDI. Cai (1999, p. 856) cites evidence that shows by the end of 1996, the cumulative stock of China's FDI abroad was amongst the largest of all developing economies, next only to Hong Kong, Singapore and Taiwan. McKibbin and Tang (2000, p. 980) quote World Bank data in asserting that in 1995 China was already the eighth largest capital supplier in the world and the largest one among developing countries. Nevertheless, the data presented in Table 7.6 still shows that when compared with foreign investment in China, the total level of Chinese investment abroad remained small, averaging less than 1 percent of GDP during the 1990s. This is indicative of the fact that there has been extremely little liberalization with respect to Chinese investment abroad. For example, residents (except for financial institutions permitted to engage in foreign borrowing) are not permitted to purchase securities and bonds abroad.

Loans to overseas entities may only be extended by financial institutions that have been approved by the SAFE and are subject to foreign currency asset–liability requirements. Foreign exchange is provided for FDI abroad only after a SAFE review of foreign exchange assets and an assessment of the investment risk involved, approval by MOFTEC and registration of the investment with SAFE (IMF, *AREAER 1998*, pp. 215, 216).

However, as was the case with respect to foreign commercial loan inflows, there is much evidence to suggest that domestic investors have been able to circumvent capital controls. Gunter (1996, p. 90) contends that actual Chinese investment abroad may have been up to six times greater than the official amount approved by the central government. The bulk of these funds have been moved abroad through the deliberate misinvoicing of imports and exports and utilizing connections with the freer financial system of Hong Kong (Gunter, 1996, pp. 81, 84). The real extent of Chinese investment abroad can be gauged by combining official figures on investment abroad with estimates of capital flight. The term capital flight is typically used to describe the unreported private accumulation of foreign assets (Eggerstedt et al., 1995, p. 211). Calculating capital flight is also a useful way to determine the overall extent of EFL in China. If significant EFL had been undertaken, domestic surplus units would be free to move funds abroad and hence such transactions would be captured by official balance of payments statistics.

Numerous methods have been proposed to measure capital flight, each of which has its advantages and limitations (see Eggerstedt et al., 1995 for a discussion). In this chapter, the conventional 'residual approach' is used, which is often associated with the BIS and the World Bank. The residual approach calculates capital flight (CF) as the difference between a country's actual foreign borrowing (FB) and its 'necessary' foreign borrowing (FB*). That is:

$$CF = FB - FB^* \qquad (7.1)$$

If FB > FB*, then it is assumed that the difference represents capital flight or, more precisely, the additional borrowing undertaken to offset capital flight (Gunter, 1996, p. 78). The extent to which a country must necessarily borrow from abroad is determined by its current account position, changes in reserves and net foreign direct investment. For example, a current account surplus, a decrease in reserves and positive net foreign direct investment will all reduce the extent to which a country must borrow from abroad. Estimates of capital flight using this approach are presented in Table 7.7. The results indicate large volumes of unofficial Chinese investment abroad, far in excess of officially recorded capital outflows. Not surprisingly, capital flight seemed to have peaked during 1997, which corresponded to the Asian financial crisis.

Table 7.7   Capital flight from China

	$US million	% GDP
1984	4 247	1.37
1985	–1 021	–0.33
1986	3 436	1.16
1987	8 767	2.73
1988	3 264	0.81
1989	1 234	0.27
1990	10 288	2.65
1991	8 942	2.20
1992	24 571	5.08
1993	23 562	3.92
1994	22 803	4.20
1995	75 569	10.79
1996	87 741	10.75
1997	132 374	14.74
1998	86 739	9.04
1999	60 921	6.16

Sources:
1.   Gunter, 1996, p. 79.
2.   IMF, *BOPS* various years.
3.   World Bank, *GDF* various years.

THE EXTENT OF EXTERNAL FINANCIAL LIBERALIZATION: EVIDENCE FROM THE EXCHANGE RATE AND CAPITAL CONTROLS

The large volumes of capital flight presented in Table 7.7 are indicative of limited EFL and suggest that capital controls remain in place. In this section the extent of EFL in China is considered further. Another way to gauge the extent of EFL that has occurred is to examine whether the value of the official exchange rate has come to reflect its equilibrium or free market value. If significant EFL had taken place, then the official exchange rate would be forced to converge to equilibrium levels by mobile international capital flows. The only way the official exchange rate can remain apart from its equilibrium value for prolonged periods of time is if capital controls are both present and effective.

An estimate of China's equilibrium exchange over time has been undertaken by Chou and Shih (1998). They derive RMB/$US exchange rates based on two theoretical models of equilibrium exchange rates; one on purchasing power parity (PPP) and the other on the shadow price of foreign exchange (SPFE). The theory behind the PPP exchange rate is well known and argues that movements in relative prices in domestic and foreign countries determine long-run exchange rates. The shadow price of foreign exchange seeks to determine the true opportunity cost to the domestic economy of acquiring an additional unit of foreign exchange (Thirlwall, 1989, p. 219). The official exchange rate in developing countries often does not reflect the true opportunity cost in light of barriers to trade and capital flows. Table 7.8 presents the official exchange rate (column 2) along with the percentage deviation from the estimated PPP rate (column 3) and SPFE rate (column 4) over the period 1978–94. This shows that while both measures suggest that the official exchange rate was initially overvalued, the deviation from equilibrium has diminished over time. By the 1990s, both series indicate that the deviation has been less than 10 percent.

Another estimate of the equilibrium RMB exchange rate can be gained by observing the officially sanctioned swap foreign exchange markets and the illegal black market for foreign exchange. Beginning in 1985, by 1994 there were 110 swap markets established in China's major cities (Chai, 1998, p. 145). While entry to these markets was initially restricted, the rate of exchange was nonetheless determined by market forces and indicated significant overvaluation of the official exchange rate during the 1980s. During the period 1987–88, the difference between the swap market rate and the official rate reached almost 80 percent. Following official devaluations in 1989–90, the degree of overvaluation narrowed to approximately 11 percent (Gunter, 1996, p. 92). However, during the latter part of 1992 the differential again widened, reaching approximately 33 percent during 1993 (Chai, 1998, p. 145). In 1994 the government abandoned the concept of differing official and swap market rates, and allowed the official rate to be unified with the depreciated swap market rate. Ding (1998, p. 35) also notes that the official exchange rate has converged with the black market exchange rate over time. For example, over the period 1988–94 the black market rate in Shanghai was anywhere between 10–200 percent greater than the official exchange rate. However, during 1994–96 the difference was negligible and subsequently the volume of funds exchanged on the black market has dwindled in size.

These observations are indicative of either significant EFL or sizeable illegal capital flows forcing the authorities to set official exchange rates at more realistic levels. The evidence favors the latter interpretation. The fact that official exchange rate reform in 1994 saw the official exchange rate being depreciated to the same level as in the swap and black markets serves as evidence that the authorities were forced to take into account equilibrium conditions (Ding, 1998, p. 41). Large volumes of illegal capital flows abroad

Table 7.8   *Official and estimated equilibrium exchange rates in China (RMB/$US)*

	Official	% deviation from PPP	% deviation from SPFE
1978	1.5571	56.66	8.89
1979	1.4962	54.63	6.46
1980	1.5303	50.70	6.74
1981	1.7455	40.13	8.56
1982	1.9227	34.09	7.83
1983	1.9809	32.52	7.57
1984	2.7957	5.09	9.52
1985	3.2015	3.34	9.37
1986	3.7221	−1.95	6.14
1987	3.7221	3.71	5.42
1988	3.7221	17.03	4.69
1989	4.7221	5.04	5.09
1990	5.2221	−7.30	3.89
1991	5.4342	−6.65	3.49
1992	5.7518	−4.34	3.05
1993	5.8000	8.76	2.74
1994	8.4462	−7.55	2.14

Note: The procedure used by Chou and Shih to estimate PPP exchange rates follows the standard procedure. That is, a base period is first chosen and then subsequent movements in relative prices (foreign and domestic) are used to update the exchange rate to the new time period. The procedure used to estimate SPFE exchange rates is more involved and the interested reader should consult Chou and Shih, 1998, pp. 170–172.

Source: Chou and Shih, 1998, pp. 170, 173.

have already been documented in Table 7.7. In addition, the IMF publishes qualitative information concerning whether its member countries employ restrictions on capital transactions. Table 7.9 summarizes this information with respect to China in 2000 and reveals that capital controls remain highly prominent. Column 1 lists various types of capital transactions. Column 2 indicates whether such transactions are subject to controls. Column 3 shows the percentage of total IMF members that have controls over that particular type of capital transaction.

Table 7.9   Controls on capital transactions, 2000

Transaction type	China	% Total (*n*=186)
Capital market securities	Yes	69
Money market instruments	Yes	60
Collective investment securities	Yes	55
Derivatives and other instruments	Yes	45
Commercial credits	Yes	59
Financial credits	Yes	61
Guarantees, sureties, and financial backup facilities	Yes	52
Direct investment	Yes	78
Liquidation of direct investment	Yes	31
Real estate transactions	Yes	74
Personal capital transactions	Yes	50

Source: IMF, *AREAER 2001*, pp. 1038, 1039.

WHY ISN'T CHINA A NET CAPITAL IMPORTER?

One interesting observation to flow from the preceding descriptive analysis is that once estimates for unofficial Chinese investment abroad are added to the official statistics, the total amount of Chinese investment abroad has, if anything, been greater than foreign investment in China. Chai (1994) and Lardy (1995) have already noted that China has not been a large net capital importer. This is a surprising result because it indicates that government-induced distortions in international capital flows are substantial. According to economic theory, if capital could flow freely, one would expect China to be a large net capital importer. This is because, given that China is a labor abundant country with a low capital/labor ratio, additional units of capital should exhibit a high marginal productivity. It is a standard economic proposition that the scarcer is one factor of production in relation to another, the higher its productivity, other things being equal (Thirlwall, 1989, p. 116). There are two types of distortions that could have led to the observed result. First, the slow pace of EFL may have restricted the extent to which foreign capital has been able to enter China. Second, government intervention in the domestic economy may have induced an artificially high outflow of Chinese capital abroad.

Evidence of high Chinese capital outflows abroad has already been documented in this study along with others (Gunter, 1996; Sicular, 1998). In this section, available data are analysed to gauge if there is any evidence to suggest that the slow pace of EFL has restricted the extent to which foreign debt has entered China. Wei (1996) has already provided evidence that FDI inflows have been less than could be expected in a liberalized environment. Therefore, this research focuses on foreign debt inflows. Testing to see whether foreign debt has been restricted is an important endeavor for two reasons. First, if there were evidence that foreign capital inflows have been restricted, one of the reasons that China has not been a large net capital importer, as expected, would be better understood. Second, restricted foreign capital inflows also imply that potentially productive investment projects have not been able to attain funding, to the detriment of economic development.

One way these issues can be examined empirically is by evaluating whether China has under-borrowed from abroad. For example, if China's actual level of foreign debt is less than some theoretical optimum level, then this would suggest that China has under-borrowed from abroad and serve as evidence that the slow pace of EFL has restricted foreign capital inflows. Empirical investigations in the literature that seek to determine a country's optimum levels of foreign borrowing can be grouped according to two different theoretical frameworks. The first utilizes an optimization approach and typically seeks to determine how much a country should borrow based on the inter-temporal maximization of a social welfare function. Despite the strong theoretical underpinnings of the optimization approach, it has rarely been utilized by policy makers in developing countries, or international financial organizations such as the IMF and World Bank, because many important variables and parameters in these models are generally not directly observable, or difficult to estimate empirically. Gemmell (1988, pp. 198–203) seeks to overcome this shortcoming by specifying a simple, two-period debt model that incorporates an optimization framework while relying on readily accessible data. A country is deemed to be maximizing a utility function (U) of the form:

$$U = C_1^\alpha + C_2^{1-\alpha} \tag{7.2}$$

where α is a parameter that depicts a society's relative preference for current (C_1) and future consumption (C_2). On the basis of this utility function, a country's optimal level of borrowing relative to GDP, $\overline{B}$, is derived as being equal to

$$\overline{B} = \frac{\phi\{\gamma(\pi_d + \pi_f) - r\}}{e\{(1+r)(1+\phi) - \phi\gamma\pi_f\}} \tag{7.3}$$

The parameter ϕ in equation (7.3) is calculated as being equal to $(1 - \alpha)/\alpha$. Therefore, the greater the ϕ, the greater the preference for future consumption. Gemmell (1988, p. 207) suggests that because α could reasonably be expected to lie between $0.2 < \alpha < 0.8$, ϕ could plausibly take a value between $4 < \phi < 0.25$. If $\phi = 1$, then this would indicate that a society had an equal preference for current and future consumption. The parameter γ in equation (7.3) is the marginal product of capital, $\Delta Y/\Delta K \equiv \delta/\pi$, where δ is the growth rate of domestic resources (real GDP) and π is the investment/GDP ratio. The parameter e is the shadow exchange rate. The parameters π_d and π_f are respectively the proportions of domestic resources and foreign borrowing devoted to investment, and r is the real interest rate on foreign borrowing.

By populating this model using parameter estimates based on the Chinese context, an estimate can be made as to whether China has under-borrowed or over-borrowed from abroad. This exercise was undertaken using data covering the period 1981–98. There are no direct data available for the parameter ϕ (Table 7.10, column 2). However, given that during the reform period China has consistently exhibited one of the highest savings rates in the world, it can be assessed that there is at least some preference for future consumption.

Table 7.10   Data and estimates of China's optimal foreign borrowing

	ϕ	γ	π_d	π_f	r	e	$\bar{B}$	B
1981	1.5	0.160	0.325	1.00	−0.086	1.9089	0.115	0.005
1982	1.5	0.274	0.332	0.91	0.103	2.0860	0.072	0.010
1983	1.5	0.322	0.338	1.00	0.181	2.1431	0.071	0.004
1984	1.5	0.442	0.344	0.59	0.067	3.0897	0.074	0.008
1985	1.5	0.357	0.378	0.34	0.145	3.5325	0.018	0.016
1986	1.5	0.233	0.377	0.38	0.183	3.9656	−0.001	0.025
1987	1.5	0.321	0.361	0.28	−0.044	3.9352	0.042	0.046
1988	1.5	0.307	0.368	0.67	0.067	3.9051	0.041	0.025
1989	1.5	0.114	0.360	1.00	0.023	4.9700	0.017	0.008
1990	1.5	0.110	0.347	0.50	−0.029	5.4332	0.014	0.023
1991	1.5	0.264	0.348	0.74	0.084	5.6307	0.022	0.013
1992	1.5	0.392	0.362	0.28	0.092	5.9329	0.016	0.029
1993	1.5	0.312	0.433	0.32	0.057	5.9637	0.018	0.031
1994	1.5	0.306	0.412	0.27	−0.102	8.6310	0.025	0.027
1995	1.5	0.257	0.408	0.31	0.067	8.3514	0.008	0.016
1996	1.5	0.242	0.396	0.55	−0.043	8.3142	0.022	0.013
1997	1.5	0.230	0.382	0.33	0.076	8.2898	0.006	0.020
1998	1.5	0.205	0.381	0.72	0.110	8.2790	0.008	0.008

Source:
1.   See text.

Therefore, ϕ is assigned a value of 1.5, which implies that α in the underlying social utility function is equal to 0.4. The marginal product of capital γ (Table 7.10, column 3) is estimated as described above by dividing the growth rate of real GDP by the rate of investment (SSB, 1999, pp. 55, 67). The proportion of domestic resources devoted to investment π_d is taken to be the rate of investment (Table 7.10, column 4) (SSB, 1999, p. 67). There are also no direct data available on the proportion of foreign borrowing that is invested π_f (Table 7.10, column 5). However, an attempt to estimate this parameter was made in the following manner. Official fixed investment data are broken down into the various sources through which they were funded, including foreign investment (SSB, 1999, p. 185). This is broadly defined to include all foreign investment types such as direct investment, loans, bonds and shares (SSB, 1999, p. 242). For the purposes of this empirical exercise, it is the proportion of fixed investment that was funded through foreign borrowing (that is, predominantly loans) that needs to be isolated. Therefore, it is necessary to subtract the proportion that has been funded through non-debt creating inflows (that is, predominantly direct investment). A rough estimate of the relative importance of foreign borrowing and non-debt creating inflows can be derived from the data that describe the amount of foreign loans and direct investment actually utilized (*ACFERT* various years). A complete data series for bonds and shares is unavailable and hence these types of foreign investment were excluded from the estimation procedure. The parameter π_f can then be calculated by dividing the estimated amount of fixed investment funded through foreign borrowing by the amount of foreign borrowing actually undertaken (World Bank, *GDF* various years). In a few years, the estimated amount of fixed investment funded through foreign borrowing was actually greater than the total amount of foreign borrowing undertaken. Therefore, in these years, π_f was assigned the maximum theoretically allowable value of 1. There were also no data available on the relative size of utilized foreign loans and direct investment in 1981. Therefore, it was assumed that the 1981 ratio was equal to that which prevailed in 1982 (*ACFERT 1984*, p. 1095). The data generated by this exercise appear plausible. It suggests that during the earlier stages of the reform period the overwhelming majority of foreign borrowing was used for investment purposes. This is to be expected in light of tight central government controls and a high proportion of official creditors. It also shows that the proportion was high in 1989 and 1998. As mentioned earlier, these were two years of known recentralization in the control of foreign loans. In contrast, π_f fell during the early 1990s as the control over foreign loans was decentralized. Following from Gemmell (1988, p. 207), the real interest rate on foreign borrowing r (Table 7.10, column 6) is estimated by subtracting the percentage change in the dollar price of China's exports from the average nominal interest rate specified on debt contracts. The average nominal interest rate is readily obtainable (World Bank, *GDF*, various years). In the absence of an official export price index, one must be constructed using export quantity and value data. To make such a task manageable, price changes were only calculated for a basket of goods that have represented China's major exports. The basket includes aquatic products, cereals (grain), vegetables, coal, crude oil, rolled steel, cotton cloth, garments and shoes. A time series of the quantity and value of these goods exported are found in China's customs statistics (SSO, 1990, pp. 444–453; SSB, *CSY*, various years). Quantity data for shoes are not available for 1980, or for garments and shoes in 1997 and 1998, and hence these goods have been omitted from the basket in these respective years. The shadow exchange rate *e* (Table 7.10, column 7) for 1980–94 is sourced from the calculations undertaken by Chou and Shih (1998, p. 173). The authors showed that by the 1990s, the difference between the estimated shadow exchange rate and the official exchange rate was minimal. Therefore, from 1995–98, *e* is assumed to equal the official exchange rate (IMF, *IFS*, various years).

On the basis of these parameter estimates, optimal borrowing $\bar{B}$ is calculated using equation (7.3) (Table 7.10, column 8). China's actual borrowing as a percentage of GNP *B* is also presented based on World Bank data (Table 7.10, column 9) (World Bank, *GDF*, various years).

While the results of optimal borrowing models should be read with caution due to the need to estimate and assume values for some data, over the entire period the results are indicative of under-borrowing. The estimated optimal borrowing levels averaged 3.3 percent of GDP while actual borrowing levels averaged just 1.8 percent for the entire period. Therefore, on the whole, the results are supportive of the hypothesis that the slow pace of EFL has restricted the extent to which foreign capital has been able to enter China, and at least partly explains why China has not been a large net capital importer. It also should be noted that the extent of under-borrowing has varied over time. It was at its most profuse during the earlier stages of the reform period, before narrowing significantly from 1985 onwards (Figure 7.1). In some periods, such as 1992–95, China's actual foreign borrowing exceeded optimal borrowing levels. These findings imply that in more recent times the major reason that China has not been a large net capital importer is because domestic financial restrictions have led to capital flight abroad.

The second approach used in the literature to determine whether a county's external borrowings are appropriate or not is based on theoretical notions of debt sustainability. This approach tracks changes in a country's foreign debt obligations, along with the capacity to repay those obligations, and so aims to consider whether foreign debt has become more or less sustainable (McDonald, 1982, p. 603). While the sustainability approach has the disadvantage of not actually specifying a particular level of debt that should be targeted, it has been

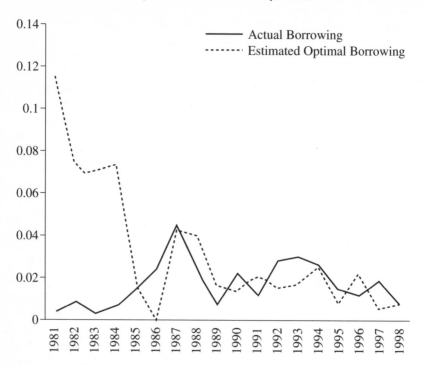

Figure 7.1   Optimal foreign borrowing versus actual foreign borrowing (% GDP)

far more widely utilized by policy makers because the required information is readily available. Examining the sustainability of a country's foreign borrowing can serve as a useful complement to optimizing approaches in determining whether a country has under-borrowed or over-borrowed. For example, given that a country such as China is likely to have a vast need for foreign capital, if actual foreign debt increased at a slower/faster rate than the capacity to repay debt, then this would be indicative of under-borrowing/over-borrowing.

The theoretical conditions for sustainable borrowing can be derived in terms of the familiar two-gap model, which states that foreign capital inflows can promote economic development by allowing a country to invest more than it saves, thereby filling a savings–investment gap, or import more than it exports, thereby filling a foreign exchange gap. If the foreign exchange gap is binding, then foreign capital inflows promote growth by increasing the amount of imports. In any period, the increase in debt due to this inflow is equal to (equations (7.4)–(7.7) are from Fishlow, 1986, p. 221 and Gillis et al., 1996, pp. 414)

$$\frac{dD}{dt} = iD + M - E \qquad (7.4)$$

where D is the stock of debt at any time, dD/dt is the change in the stock of debt with respect to time, i is the average interest rate on foreign capital inflows, M is the value of imports and E is the value of exports. The differential equation (7.4) can be solved to show that under a foreign exchange gap, the long-run equilibrium ratio of debt to exports will equal

$$\frac{D}{E} = \frac{a}{(g_E - i)} \qquad (7.5)$$

where a is the ratio of the foreign exchange gap to exports, $(M - E)/E$, and g_E is the growth rate of exports. Equation (7.5) states that for a given foreign exchange gap, there is an equilibrium ratio of debt to exports that can be sustained. If export growth, g_E is greater than the interest rate i, then the ratio of debt to exports will fall. The key then to sustaining debt under a foreign exchange gap is to ensure that foreign capital inflows are put to uses that either directly or indirectly boost exports.

If it is the savings–investment gap that is binding, then foreign capital inflows boost growth by increasing the amount of investment. In this case, in any period the increase in debt due to this inflow is equal to

$$\frac{dD}{dt} = iD + I - S_d = iD + vY - sY = iD + (v - s)Y \qquad (7.6)$$

where Y is GNP, v is the investment share of GNP, and s is the propensity to save out of GNP. Equation (7.6) can be solved to show that under a savings–investment gap, the long-run equilibrium ratio of debt to GNP will be equal to

$$\frac{D}{Y} = \frac{(v - s)}{(g_Y - i)} \qquad (7.7)$$

Equation (7.7) states that for a given savings–investment gap, there is an equilibrium ratio of debt to GDP that can be sustained. It also shows that the key to sustaining debt under a savings–investment gap is to ensure that foreign capital inflows are directed towards activities that are productive enough to ensure that the growth rate of GNP, g_Y, will at least be equal to i.

Table 7.11 presents the relevant data necessary to determine the sustainability of China's debt during the reform period. The data shows that g_Y, g_E and i have averaged 7.8 percent, 15.1 percent and 6.9 percent respectively. Thus,

Table 7.11   The sustainability of China's foreign debt

	g_Y	g_E	i
1980	16.1	32.7	10.3
1981	−5.4	21.5	8.2
1982	−1.9	1.4	7.0
1983	7.4	−0.4	7.2
1984	2.6	17.4	7.5
1985	−0.9	4.8	7.5
1986	−3.2	13.1	6.4
1987	8.8	27.5	6.6
1988	24.8	20.5	7.2
1989	12.0	10.6	7.3
1990	−13.6	18.2	7.5
1991	4.8	15.7	6.1
1992	18.9	18.2	6.2
1993	24.4	8.0	5.5
1994	−9.7	31.9	5.5
1995	29.1	22.9	6.5
1996	16.6	1.5	6.6
1997	10.0	21.0	6.5
1998	6.8	0.5	6.2

Note: Growth rates calculated in this table were based on $US estimates of GNP and exports.

Source: World Bank, *GDF*, various years.

the conditions for sustainable borrowing have been more than met. This result is supportive of the earlier evidence attained using the optimization approach and suggests that China has under-borrowed from abroad. The fact that g_Y, $g_E > i$ means that China has an extremely low level of external debt by international standards. For example, in 1998 the ratio of China's debt to exports and GNP was 72.4 percent and 16.4 percent respectively. For a comparison with other large developing countries, the same ratios for Brazil were 358.9 percent and 30.6 percent, and for India, 167.2 percent and 23.0 percent (World Bank, *GDF 2000*, pp. 122, 162, 290). While there are no firm critical levels that constitute dangerous debt levels, on the basis of country experience with debt servicing the World Bank has established some rough guidelines. If a country has either a ratio of present value of debt service to GNP (PV/Y) of greater than 80 percent, or if the ratio of the present value of debt service to exports (PV/E) is greater than 220 percent, it is classified as severely indebted. If 48 percent < PV/Y < 80 percent or 132 percent < PV/E < 220 percent, then the country is classified as moderately indebted. If PV/Y < 48 percent and PV/E < 132 percent then the country is assigned the most creditworthy ranking of less indebted (World Bank, *GDF 1996*, p. 42). Over the period 1996–98, PV/Y and PV/E in China averaged just 15 percent and 67 percent respectively (World Bank, *GDF 2000*, p. 147).

THEORETICAL ASPECTS OF EXTERNAL FINANCIAL LIBERALIZATION AND POLICY IMPLICATIONS FOR CHINA

The previous section revealed evidence of China under-borrowing from abroad. The implication is that the slow pace of EFL has meant that some potentially productive investment projects have not been able to attract funding. However, this finding does not automatically mean that China's economic development would be best served by immediately embarking on an accelerated program of EFL. This is because the sequencing of economic reforms in a developing, transitional economy such as China plays an important role in determining whether the development impact of EFL will be a positive one (Eichengreen et al., 1998, p. 10). The first prerequisite necessary for successful EFL is fiscal reform. According to McKinnon (1993, p. 8), fiscal reform is a necessary prerequisite for all other reforms in a transitional economy. If a government cannot secure fiscal integrity, it must finance revenue shortfalls through printing money and/or compelling SOBs to engage in rapid credit creation. This fuels inflation, which has well known negative implications for macroeconomic stability and microeconomic efficiency. The most recently conducted comprehensive study of China's fiscal system indicates that much work still remains to be done in the area of fiscal reform (Wong et al., 1995).

A second prerequisite reform is that DFL should be undertaken prior to EFL (McKinnon, 1993, p. 9). There are several reasons for this. First, if domestic interest rates are still repressed at below equilibrium levels, EFL can lead to a perverse capital outflow as domestic surplus units react to artificially low returns at home and seek higher returns abroad. Second, DFL exposes the prudential framework surrounding a country's financial markets and institutions to testing in a market-driven environment and signals whether improvements are necessary. Without an adequate prudential framework, liberalized financial systems become vulnerable to the effects of market failure. Indeed, numerous authors have cited financial liberalization outpacing the capacity of prudential frameworks as a key factor underlying the Asian financial crisis (Corsetti et al., 1999, p. 1234). If the prudential framework of a country cannot ensure the prudent and efficient use of domestic savings, post-DFL, then it will have little hope with respect to foreign savings, post-EFL. McKinnon and Pill (1996, p. 22) note that EFL poses numerous challenges for the prudential framework over and above those posed by DFL. These include the exchange rate risk on international borrowing and the danger that foreign lenders may seek to take advantage of the fact that the domestic government generally guarantees the liabilities of domestic financial institutions. Third, DFL exposes domestic financial institutions to competitive pressures and forces them to change their behavior accordingly. Without this stepping-stone, they would unlikely be able to deal with the rigors of international competition bought on by EFL. This is especially the case for financial institutions in transitional economies, where staff have traditionally been concerned with simply implementing a centrally promulgated credit plan and have acquired few technical skills and experience in areas such as risk assessment, risk management and profit maximization. Fourthly, if the government continues to intervene in the credit allocation and pricing decisions of domestic financial institutions, they will be unable to effectively compete with foreign financial institutions. Although significant progress has been made in China with respect to DFL, several key aspects remain unresolved (Laurenceson and Chai, 1998; Lardy, 1998a). For one, the government continues to intervene in the operations of SOBs and they have yet to be restructured to the point where they could effectively compete with foreign financial institutions. Second, the adequacy of China's prudential framework to deal with a market-driven financial system is also questionable. The experience of China's NBFIs are a case in point.

A third reform that may be considered necessary before a country undertakes EFL is the adoption of a more flexible exchange rate system. It should be noted, however, that the necessity of this reform is not universally accepted. IMF (1994, p. 3), for example, concludes that the type of exchange rate regime appears not to be a critical factor in successfully conducting capital account liberalization. Nevertheless, this issue has attracted increased attention in light of the Asian crisis, where several of the crisis economies conducted EFL in the presence of a fixed exchange rate regime. The fundamental problem with removing capital controls under a fixed exchange rate regime is that monetary independence is lost, which can result in large fluctuations in output. While the forces of demand and supply nominally determine the exchange rate in China, in reality the system offers limited flexibility. For example, the daily movement of the RMB against the US dollar is limited to 0.3 percent on either side of the reference rate announced by the PBC at the start of each day's trading (IMF, *AREAER 2001*, p. 212). The central bank and SOBs regularly intervene in the foreign currency market to maintain stability. Tsang (1997, p. 241) reports on Chinese research that estimated the Bank of China was responsible for 70–80 percent of the foreign currency sold in the inter-bank market for foreign exchange, while the PBC was responsible for 70–80 percent of the foreign currency bought.

CONCLUSION

The topic of EFL in China has only been scantily covered in the existing literature. This chapter began by investigating the nature of EFL that has taken place during the reform period. It was shown that while some EFL can be identified with respect to capital flows such as inward FDI, most other types of international capital flows, particularly Chinese investment abroad, remains tightly controlled. The limited overall extent of EFL was also confirmed by evidence of large volumes of unofficial capital flight exiting China and documented controls over capital transactions.

The empirical investigation conducted in this chapter revealed evidence that the slow pace of EFL has restricted foreign debt inflows into China. This is an important finding because it suggests that some potentially productive investment opportunities have gone unrealized. However, before an accelerated program of EFL can be looked upon as a development promoting strategy, the wider literature cautions that several prerequisite reforms must first be conducted. In the case of China, the most pressing reforms first needed are fiscal reform and further DFL. It is also likely that greater levels of EFL would need to be accompanied by increased exchange rate flexibility.

8. Conclusion

MAJOR FINDINGS

The major findings of this research can be summarized according to two central themes. First, when viewed in a historical perspective, the Chinese financial sector has experienced substantial reform since the transition to a market economy began in 1978. Particularly prominent in this liberalization has been vast institutional diversification. Prior to 1978, China's financial system consisted almost exclusively of a state-owned, mono-banking system. Early in the reform period this system was replaced with a two-tiered banking structure, with the PBC installed as the central bank and other SOBs performing a mix of development and commercial banking functions. Banks of various other ownership classifications have also joined the SOBs. In addition to banking system institutional diversification, numerous NBFIs have emerged including UCCs, TICs, the postal savings network, finance companies, insurance companies, leasing companies and securities companies. Direct capital markets for both equity and debt are also now part of the modern Chinese financial system.

Another prominent aspect of financial sector reform has been that government controls over financial institutions have been relaxed. Prior to the transition to a market economy, financial institutions were directly controlled by the central government, interest rates were fixed at low levels, and the volume and direction of credit was decreed in a detailed manner by the credit plan. However, during the reform period, a floating interest rate system has been introduced, which has given financial institutions varying degrees of autonomy to set their own interest rates within a specified band around official interest rates. Furthermore, even during periods of high inflation, real long-term deposit interest rates remained positive through the linking of the official nominal interest rate paid on savings deposits to changes in the overall retail price index. Apart from periods of macroeconomic austerity, over time the details of the credit plan have also became more indicative in nature rather than binding. In addition, the coverage of the credit plan lessened over time, as many of the emerging financial institutions such as NBFIs were not strictly incorporated into the plan.

Finally, the means through which the PBC influences the activities of financial institutions has become more indirect and in line with international norms. There are no longer any financial institutions still subject to direct credit ceilings. Rather, control over financial institutions is now chiefly exercised indirectly through asset–liability management principles that operate along similar lines to those found in more developed, market economies. The control of financial institutions has also experienced greater decentralization as local branch managers and loan officers have acquired increased discretion rather than simply passively implementing the directives of the central government.

The second major finding of this research is that, on the whole, financial sector reform has positively contributed to China's economic development. This conclusion is based upon two key factors. For one, the empirical evidence suggests that financial sector reform has helped facilitate the mobilization of a large volume of savings to fund investment. The combination of increased interest rate flexibility and the indexation of official deposit interest rates has meant that the incentive for surplus agents to hold financial savings has been maintained. Furthermore, the institutional diversification that has taken place has led to increased financial institution density, thus lowering the transaction costs associated with surplus agents accessing the formal financial system. Various non-state banks and NBFIs providing financial services to areas that have traditionally been poorly served by the state banking system, such as in rural regions and the non-state sector have extended the reach of the formal financial system. An econometric analysis confirmed the leading role played by the real deposit rate of interest and financial institution density in the rapid financial deepening that has occurred in China during the reform period. An interesting observation flowing from this finding is that complete interest rate liberalization is not a necessary prerequisite for financial deepening. Rather, what is of more fundamental importance is that if interest rates continue to be regulated, they should be set at levels sufficient to maintain the incentive of surplus agents to hold financial assets. The success of China in regulating interest rates while maintaining positive returns is similar to that of many of the other rapidly developing Asian economies (World Bank, 1993a, p. 205; Stiglitz and Uy, 1996, pp. 252–254). To the extent that numerous studies have also demonstrated that a robust relationship exists between financial depth and economic growth (Levine, 1997), such financial reforms in China are likely to have contributed to the rapid economic growth experienced during the reform period.

Second, on balance the evidence suggests that financial reform has assisted in the channeling of savings to relatively more productive investments. Data limitations not withstanding, an econometric analysis suggested that during the reform period, investment that had been funded through domestic loans displayed a relatively high marginal productivity when compared with investment funded through other means. This finding is consistent with the results of several other recent studies that have sort to gauge the productivity of the various investment funding sources in China using both national and provincial level data. It is also in accordance with the results of recent microeconomic studies that have shown the TFP of SOEs has been increasing and that SOBs have lent to relatively productive SOEs. Several aspects regarding financial reform can be identified as having contributed to this outcome. First, there is evidence that the gradual approach to financial reform has reduced the scope for widespread market failure to occur. The conceptual argument had already been made by several prominent authors that wholesale financial liberalization in a transitional environment where fiscal, enterprise and pricing reforms remain incomplete, is likely to worsen allocative efficiency in lending rather than improve it. Second, financial reform has given financial institutions more discretion in their lending decisions. Importantly, this increased discretion has often been complemented by other incentive reforms such as the linking of a loan officer's remuneration with the performance of their loan portfolio. Third, financial reform has resulted in improvements in areas such as accounting and disclosure standards, making it easier for financial institutions and individual investors to identify efficient and profitable firms. Finally, available empirical evidence suggests that the institutional diversification that has characterized financial reform in China has also served to improve the allocative efficiency of lending. While SOBs have been lending to relatively productive SOEs, the emerging non-state banks and NBFIs have been prominent in meeting the financial needs of the rapidly growing non-state sector.

While the overall finding that financial reform has promoted economic development appears robust, it important to note that there are some costs and dangers that can be identified in the Chinese approach to financial reform. For one, available empirical evidence suggests that too little attention has been paid to strengthening the prudential framework surrounding financial institutions. This threatens the solvency of such financial institutions and jeopardizes the positive and sustainable impact of the financial sector on economic development in the long run. One of the dangers of a gradual approach to financial reform is that traditional moral hazard problems in firms and financial institutions remain unresolved, which places tremendous pressure on regulatory and supervisory systems to keep such negative behavior in check. Of course, it should also be remembered that moral hazard is not a problem unique to the gradual approach and can plague even financial systems that are fully liberalized. Second, a gradual approach to financial reform can also reduce the incentive for other necessary reforms to be completed. For example, the Chinese government has essentially been able to use the savings of the household sector deposited in SOBs to compensate for a lack of fiscal reform. The end cost of this approach cannot yet be fully ascertained, although the potential danger to financial institution solvency is very real. Finally, the empirical evidence suggested that the usage of the stock market solely for the purposes of SOE reform has been ineffective, at least when combined with a continuing commitment to majority state ownership.

POLICY IMPLICATIONS FOR OTHER TRANSITIONAL ECONOMIES

The superior economic performance of China to date in its transition to a market economy when compared with other transitional economies such as those in Central and Eastern Europe has been well established. The single most glaring difference is that whereas China has managed to maintain relative macroeconomic stability, nearly all other transitional economies have been seriously affected by rampant inflation. For example, IMF (1999, pp. 155, 157) shows that over the period 1991–98, inflation in China averaged 9.5 percent annually, compared with 130 percent in the transitional economies of Central and Eastern Europe. Therefore, largely as a result of this divergence in macroeconomic stability, the average growth rate of real GDP over the same period in China was 10.8 percent, compared with –2.0 percent in the transitional economies of Central and Eastern Europe. The relative macroeconomic stability achieved by China has also contributed to rapid financial development and stability. Again, this is in contrast with most transitional economies. Gorton and Winton (1998), for example, note that financial sector reform in most transitional economies has gone hand in hand with increased instability and virtually all have experienced some sort of banking crisis. These findings are corroborated by Scholtens (2000), who also shows that the financial sector in most transitional economies remains shallow. What lessons then does the Chinese approach to financial reform hold for other transitional economies?

The general lesson that the Chinese experience offers to other transitional economies is that there are benefits to be gained by maintaining some government intervention in the financial sector during the transitional period. Under this general theme, numerous specific examples and policy lessons can be cited. First, in order to maintain macroeconomic stability during the transition to a market economy, the pace of financial reform must be coordinated with progress in the area of fiscal reform. The transition to a market economy intrinsically erodes the government's fiscal position, with the end result typically being escalating inflation as fiscal deficits are monetized. The first best solution to this problem is to place reform of the fiscal system at the very beginning of the transitional program. The reality is that most transitional economies, including China, have been unable to successfully do so. What the Chinese experience illustrates is that coordinating financial reform with fiscal reform can represent a second best, albeit temporary, alternative. The combination of maintaining positive real interest rates on savings in the state banking system and limiting alternative financial asset choices has meant that the Chinese government has been able to absorb the excess liquidity of the household sector, and at the same time collect seigniorage revenue to help fund fiscal expenditure obligations. Essentially excluding the non-state sector from accessing investment funding through the SOBs has also eased inflationary pressures. Therefore, if either sufficient fiscal reform is not first conducted, or if the pace of financial reform is not coordinated with the progress in fiscal reform, then extremely high rates of inflation can be the expected outcome. The combination of superior macroeconomic stability and the maintenance of positive real interest rates has also meant that the Chinese financial sector has greatly outperformed other transitional economies in terms of mobilizing funds for investment. World Bank (1996, pp. 99–101), for example, reports that although most transitional economies had a similar level of financial depth during the late 1980s, by the mid-1990s China's financial depth was more than double that of the transitional economies in Central and Eastern Europe.

Second, the largely positive impact of financial reform on economic development in China lends empirical support to the theory of McKinnon (1991) and Long and Sagari (1991) that the pace of financial reform is dependent upon, and should be coordinated with, the degree of enterprise reform. This is in contrast to some reformers and transitional economies that have tried to first install a market financial system in the hope that it would force enterprise reform. Complete financial liberalization is more likely to frustrate economic development rather than promote it if firms continue to possess a soft budget constraint. This is because such firms do not respond to price signals and will simply continue to borrow whenever possible and bid up the interest rate to unsustainable levels. Also, as long as firms and banks possess a soft budget constraint, cancelling the debts of firms and recapitalizing the banks is unlikely to change their behavior. World Bank (1996, p. 102) reports that in Bulgaria and Romania, where large-scale debt forgiveness was undertaken prior to sufficient enterprise reform, unprofitable enterprises continued to borrow rather than adjust their behavior. These perverse incentives have contributed to the fact that banks in many transitional economies have actually experienced an increase in the proportion of NPLs after greater financial liberalization (Griffith-Jones, 1995, p. 9; World Bank, 1996, p. 99; Borish et al., 1997, p. 343; Gorton and Winton, 1998; Scholtens, 2000, p. 541).

Third, the Chinese experience with financial reform suggests that the pace of financial liberalization must be tied to the development of the prudential framework surrounding financial institutions and markets. This policy lesson has often emerged from China's failures in this area. The high level of NPLs in many non-state-owned financial institutions in China, including foreign banks, serves as evidence that merely breaking the cycle of SOBs' lending to SOEs is not sufficient to ensure that financial liberalization will improve financial performance or allocative efficiency. Even financial institutions in mature, market economies have an incentive to take excessive risks because the government typically provides some form of deposit insurance. Thus, the development of an effective prudential framework is a necessary condition for successful financial liberalization. The view that hardening budget constraints is not a substitute for effective prudential regulation and supervision is consistent with the experience of other transitional economies. Griffith-Jones (1995, p. 9), for example, reports that in the case of Poland after financial liberalization, '...the deterioration in the portfolio quality of private banks has been as rapid, if not more so, than in state banks'. Similarly, Griffith-Jones and FitzGerald (1995, p. 225) report that in the Czech Republic, Hungary and Poland, '...new banks – which are more aggressive in their lending practices, and often have lower initial levels of provisions – seem to be becoming more exposed to bad debts than the larger, more established banks'.

Finally, the Chinese experience with financial reform during the early 1980s highlights that transitional countries must coordinate the pace of financial reforms with progress made in reforms to the price system. This is an issue that does not arise in most developing countries where the market already prices most goods and services prior to financial reform. However, in the context of a transitional economy, a partially reformed price system means that a liberalized financial system will be allocating credit based upon price signals that do not accurately reflect relative scarcities. A liberalized financial system will rationally channel credit to areas in the economy where government controls over prices are weak. However, this direction of credit need not reflect the optimal allocation of loanable funds.

POLICY IMPLICATIONS FOR THE FUTURE OF FINANCIAL REFORM IN CHINA

The policy implications of the findings of this study for the future of financial reform in China are interesting. On one hand, because overall financial reform appears to have positively impacted upon economic development, it can be concluded that past policies have had considerable merit. However, by way of conclusion, it is suggested that financial reform in China is at a new crossroads and past policies are unlikely to serve economic development well in the future. This is because numerous pressures, both internal and external to China, can be identified that will necessitate a more rapid and comprehensive approach to financial reform and indeed economic reform more generally.

First, economic theory and international experience suggests that while government intervention in the financial sector can have marked benefits in the initial stages of development, the returns diminish over time and are generally soon overshadowed by the costs of government failure (Park, 1994, p. 3; Patrick, 1994, p. 366; Hellman et al., 1997, p. 166). It is in the initial stages of economic development that market failures are greatest with poorly developed information systems and incomplete markets. However, as economies develop, information systems improve and markets become more complete, and so the benefits of government intervention decline. At the same time, greater levels of economic development imply that the economy is becoming increasingly complex and sophisticated, making it more difficult and costly for the government to micro-manage. Therefore, even though government intervention in the financial sector in the past may have helped to address market failure, the scope to continue to do so in the future will shrink. As a result, it would appear to be sound policy for China to undertake the necessary prerequisite reforms so that more extensive financial liberalization can be successfully pursued in the near future. Otherwise, the danger is that China will meet a similar fate to that experienced by some of the other high-growth Asian developing countries during the financial crisis of 1997.

Second, Lardy (1998a, p. 187) argues that China will increasingly face financial constraints to achieving sustainable economic growth in the future. He contends that addressing problem areas such as environmental degradation and inadequate infrastructure will require large amounts of investment resources. In the past, China has been able to use SOBs, financed by a rising household savings rate and seigniorage revenue derived from increased monetization, to fund the continued support of SOEs (Chai, 2000, p. XXXIX). However, given the huge need for investment resources, and the fact that the scope for further increases in the savings rate and seigniorage revenue are small, the only option will be to reform the SOBs and SOEs. A reassessment of the role played by the stock market could also be an important avenue through which financial constraints to growth can be eased. By opening up the listing process to non-state enterprises, the stock market could be placed in a more prominent position to influence the level of aggregate savings.

Third, Sachs and Woo (1997) argue that some of the sources of growth that have driven China's economic development in the past will soon be exhausted. Unlike most other transitional economies, China began its transition to a market economy with a relatively large agricultural and non-state sector. This meant that China was not forced to undertake comprehensive state sector reform immediately. Rather, it simply liberalized its agricultural and non-state sectors, thus fueling economic growth by shifting workers from the low productivity agricultural sector into the high productivity non-state sector (Chai, 2000, XXXIX). However, this source of growth cannot be sustained indefinitely, thus prompting the need for policy attention to turn to the reform of the state sector.

Finally, the need for China to undertake the necessary prerequisite reforms for successful financial liberalization is made all the more urgent in light of the fact that the pace of financial reform will increasingly be dictated by external sources such as the WTO, to which China is now a member. For example, under the WTO accession agreement document, five years after accession foreign banks will be able to freely compete with SOBs for the RMB business of domestic individuals and enterprises throughout China (*The Economist*, 8 April 2000). The proposed timetable for meeting this obligation was recently released by the PBC. Upon joining the WTO, China will cancel regional and client limitations applying to foreign banks in the handling of foreign exchange business. In addition, restrictions on foreign banks handling individual RMB business in Shenzhen, Shanghai, Dalian and Tianjin will be removed. One year after WTO entry, individual RMB business in Guangzhou, Zhuhai, Qingdao, Nanjing and Wuhan will be opened to foreign banks. Two years after, the process will be extended to Jinan, Fuzhou, Chengdu and Chongqing; three years after, Kunming, Beijing and Xiamen; fours years after, Shantou, Ningbo, Shenyang and Xian; five years after, all remaining regional restrictions will be lifted. Two years after WTO entry foreign banks will also be allowed to handle RMB business for domestic enterprises across China (*People's Daily*, 6 December 2001).

Therefore, while financial reform has positively impacted upon economic development in the past, it appears that there will need to be a substantial change in policy direction if this is to continue in a sustainable fashion into the future. Financial reform, however, cannot be conducted in isolation. Before SOEs and SOBs can be comprehensively reformed, it is first necessary for China to establish an effective fiscal revenue collection system. In this way, any continued support for the SOEs can be funded explicitly, and SOBs will be free to transform themselves into true commercial banks. Furthermore, as inefficient and/or unprofitable SOEs are closed, it will also become necessary to use the fiscal system to fund a more comprehensive social security system than the one that operates presently. After SOBs have been freed of the need to support SOEs, a recapitalization program will then be needed to lift the financial burden of past bad debts. Indeed, this process has already begun with the RMB 270 billion capital injection in 1998 and the formation of asset management companies in 2000. These companies plan to purchase about RMB1300 billion in SOB non-performing assets (*ACFB 2000*, p. 36). However, as has been shown through the experience of other transitional economies, freeing SOBs of policy lending responsibilities and the burden of past bad debts is not sufficient for ensuring that future lending will be extended prudently. This will only take place if a strengthening of the prudential framework complements the severing of the link between SOBs and SOEs and a host of other practical issues such as staff retraining are addressed. The efficiency of future lending may also be enhanced if the incentive structure facing SOBs is improved. There are numerous ways this can be done. First, a privatization program could be undertaken. Indeed the future listing of the SOBs is a topic that is already under consideration by the PBC (*People's Daily*, 10 May 2001). Alternative arrangements such as joint ventures with foreign banks may be more palatable on an ideological level in the nearer term. The PBC has already begun to use foreign companies to assist in the disposal of the non-performing assets of SOBs attained by the asset management companies (*People's Daily*, 28 December 2001). Second, SOBs could be exposed to greater levels of competition from both domestic and foreign financial institutions. Greater competition implies a move towards comprehensive DFL including full interest rate liberalization. Interest rate liberalization can only be safely undertaken after the other reforms mentioned above have first been addressed. Finally, after comprehensive DFL has been completed, China can begin to look upon greater levels of EFL as a growth enhancing policy.

Therefore, financial reform in China has reached a new juncture. Policy approaches that have had success in the past are unlikely to be sufficient for facilitating sustainable economic development in the future. Undertaking decisive policy action of the kind described above could result in the financial sector being an important engine of growth behind China's future economic development. The alternative of maintaining the status quo is likely to not only jeopardize the stability of the financial sector, but also China's successful transition to a market economy as a whole.

Appendix

Table A1   Financial depth modeling data

	FD	GDPCAP	RIR	FRI	DEN
1978	0.19	379.00	2.52	56.13	7.90
1979	0.26	402.12	1.75	55.84	8.82
1980	0.29	428.26	−0.91	54.69	10.03
1981	0.33	444.96	2.93	54.48	10.69
1982	0.35	478.33	3.70	54.26	11.12
1983	0.37	522.82	4.20	53.87	11.39
1984	0.39	594.44	2.88	50.72	12.23
1985	0.43	665.18	−1.91	51.84	13.04
1986	0.50	713.07	1.13	49.19	14.14
1987	0.54	782.95	−0.09	47.40	15.55
1988	0.50	857.33	−9.13	45.87	17.47
1989	0.54	878.77	−5.67	47.12	18.19
1990	0.65	898.98	7.76	47.09	19.07
1991	0.71	968.20	4.88	46.62	20.20
1992	0.75	1092.13	2.05	44.68	21.17
1993	0.84	1225.13	−3.35	43.86	22.78
1994	0.85	1365.06	−8.81	45.04	22.03
1995	0.90	1492.01	−3.33	44.55	22.79
1996	0.98	1617.34	2.93	44.35	23.86
1997	1.09	1741.88	6.32	46.35	24.91
1998	1.11	1858.58	7.83	46.28	25.16
1999	1.30	1973.81	4.87	46.06	26.05

Source:
1.   See text.

Table A2   Derivation of DGV (billion yuan, 1990 prices)

	GV	P_G	DGV
1980	376.16	0.5711	658.66
1981	385.95	0.5722	674.50
1982	413.32	0.5711	723.73
1983	452.40	0.5705	792.99
1984	505.42	0.5785	873.67
1985	611.49	0.6289	972.32
1986	688.82	0.6527	1055.34
1987	799.39	0.7043	1135.01
1988	994.67	0.8100	1227.99
1989	1187.30	0.9606	1236.00
1990	1257.05	1.0000	1257.05
1991	1437.17	1.0620	1353.27
1992	1709.11	1.1342	1506.89
1993	2208.80	1.4064	1570.53
1994	2530.12	1.6807	1505.40
1995	2588.99	1.9311	1340.68
1996	2728.94	1.9871	1373.33
1997	2785.86	1.9811	1406.22

Note: GV is the gross output value of SOIEs at current prices. From 1980–92 this series is sourced from Jefferson et al., 1996, p. 177. From 1993–97 it comes from SSB, 1994–1998. P_G is an ex-factory price index for industrial output conducted by the Urban Survey Team of China's State Statistical Bureau. It is published in SSB, 1999, p. 309. DGV is the gross output value of SOIEs at constant prices. It is calculated as (GV) / (P_G).

Table A3   Derivation of DNPF (billion yuan, 1990 prices)

	OF*	OPF*	GI	CC	P_K	DGI–DCC	DNPF*	DNPF
1980	373.01	311.62	16.31	13.71	0.413	6.30	496.66	493.50
1981	403.23	332.30	20.68	14.73	0.438	13.58	510.24	503.45
1982	437.54	360.73	28.43	15.94	0.440	28.39	538.63	524.43
1983	476.78	388.25	27.52	18.10	0.476	19.79	558.42	548.52
1984	516.00	419.33	31.08	20.85	0.510	20.06	578.47	568.45
1985	595.61	487.01	67.68	24.70	0.582	73.85	652.32	615.40
1986	678.55	546.17	59.16	28.73	0.666	45.69	698.01	675.17
1987	767.79	617.96	71.79	32.42	0.739	53.27	751.29	724.65
1988	879.52	712.67	94.71	37.94	0.795	71.41	822.70	786.99
1989	1016.08	825.92	113.25	43.49	0.983	70.97	893.66	858.18
1990	1161.03	946.90	120.98	48.28	1.000	72.70	966.36	930.01
1991	1355.68	1115.86	168.96	57.79	1.119	99.35	1065.71	1016.04
1992	1566.98	1288.45	172.59	68.62	1.255	82.84	1148.56	1107.13
1993	1906.64	1563.44	274.99	83.89	1.589	120.27	1268.82	1208.69
1994	2310.20	1894.36	330.92	101.65	1.754	130.71	1399.54	1399.54
1995	3093.57	2536.73	642.36	136.12	1.857	272.62	1672.15	1535.84
1996	3476.50	2850.73	314.00	152.97	1.931	83.40	1755.55	1713.85
1997	3835.10	3144.78	294.05	168.74	1.965	63.77	1819.13	1787.24

Notes: 1. OF* is the year end value of SOIEs' fixed assets, at original cost and at current prices. From 1980–88 this series is sourced from Jefferson et al., 1992, p. 245. From 1989 to 1992 it comes from Jefferson et al., 1996, p. 150. From 1993 to 1997 is comes from SSB, 1994–1998. OPF* is the year end value of SOIEs' fixed assets used for industrial production, at original cost and at current prices. The data for 1980–92 are calculated by Jefferson et al., 1996, p. 176. In 1992, they estimate that 82 percent of OF* is used for industrial production. They also show that this proportion has remained almost constant since 1980. It is therefore assumed that for the years 1993–97, OPF* equals $0.82 \times$ (OF*). GI is gross investment of SOIEs at current prices. It is calculated as the change in OPF*. CC is the annual value of capital consumption allowances at current prices. This depreciation allowance is used to calculate the net value of SOIEs' fixed investment. Jefferson et al., 1996, p. 176 attain these not readily available data for 1980–92 directly from China's State Statistical Bureau. In 1992, CC equaled 4.4 percent of (OF*). This ratio has also shown little fluctuation since 1980 and it is therefore assumed that for the years 1993–97, CC equals $0.044 \times$ (OF*). P_K is a price index for newly added fixed assets. It is used to attain the value of net fixed investment in constant prices. Until 1992, we use the fixed investment deflator constructed by Jefferson et al., 1996, p. 175. From 1993 to 1997 we use the official fixed investment deflator found in SSB, 1994–1998. DGI–DCC is the value of net investment valued at constant prices. It is calculated as $(GI)/(P_K) - (CC)/(P_K)$. DNPF* is the year end value of SOIEs' net fixed assets used for industrial production at constant prices. The initial value for this variable in 1979 is estimated in Jefferson et al., 1996, p. 176 to be 490.36. The values in following years are attained by consecutively adding (DGI – DCC). DNPF is the average value of SOIEs' net fixed assets used for industrial production at constant prices. It is computed as an arithmetic average of consecutive year end figures for (DNPF*).

Table A4 Derivation of DINT (billion yuan, 1990 prices)

	GV	NV	CC + MRF	INT	P_M	DINT
1980	376.16	131.91	21.41	222.84	0.389	572.85
1981	385.95	131.75	22.91	231.29	0.392	590.03
1982	413.32	137.29	24.94	251.09	0.396	634.07
1983	452.40	150.08	28.08	274.24	0.401	683.89
1984	505.42	172.10	32.01	301.31	0.421	715.70
1985	611.49	205.77	37.70	368.02	0.497	740.48
1986	688.82	220.73	43.76	424.33	0.545	778.59
1987	799.39	252.94	49.38	497.07	0.604	822.96
1988	994.67	306.30	57.94	630.43	0.749	841.70
1989	1187.30	346.80	66.90	773.60	0.947	816.90
1990	1257.05	356.87	75.33	824.85	1.000	824.85
1991	1437.17	401.91	89.79	945.47	1.091	866.61
1992	1709.11	483.11	106.62	1119.38	1.211	924.34
1993	2208.80	728.10	129.65	1351.05	1.636	825.82
1994	2530.12	728.10	157.09	1582.73	1.934	818.37
1995	2588.99	830.72	210.36	1547.91	2.230	694.13
1996	2728.94	874.24	236.40	1618.30	2.295	705.14
1997	2785.86	919.29	260.79	1605.78	2.288	701.83

Note: 1. GV is the same as Table A2. NV is the net output (value added) of SOIEs at current prices. From 1980 to 1992 this series is sourced from Jefferson et al., 1996, p. 177. From 1993 to 1997, it comes from SSB, 1994–1998. CC + MRF is the combined annual value of capital consumption allowances and major repair funds at current prices. These variables are required so that the accounting identity, $GV \equiv NV + INT + CC + MRF$, can be used to solve for INT. CC is the same as in Table A3. Jefferson et al., 1996, p. 177 were able attain these not readily available minor accounting data series for 1980–92 directly from China's State Statistical Bureau. In 1992, their combined value was 6.68 percent of OF^*. It is assumed this ratio remains the same for the years 1993–97. INT is the value of intermediate inputs used by SOIEs at current prices. It is equal to $(GV) - (NV) - (CC+MRF)$. P_M is a price index for intermediate inputs. It is used to attain the value of intermediate inputs at constant prices. Until 1984, the price series constructed by Jefferson et al., 1992, p. 246 is used. From 1984 to 1997 a price index for intermediate inputs used in industrial production undertaken by the Urban Survey Team of China's State Statistical Bureau is used. This index is published in the monthly journal *Zhongguo Wujia* [China Price]. DINT is the value of intermediate inputs used by SOIEs at constant prices. It is calculated as $(INT)/(P_M)$.

Table A5   *Derivation of LAB (million workers)*

	EMP	EXC	LAB
1980	31.78	0.15	27.01
1981	33.27	0.15	28.28
1982	34.55	0.15	29.37
1983	35.28	0.15	29.99
1984	35.73	0.15	30.37
1985	37.04	0.15	31.48
1986	38.85	0.15	33.02
1987	39.82	0.15	33.85
1988	41.33	0.15	35.13
1989	42.34	0.16	35.57
1990	42.94	0.16	36.07
1991	44.46	0.16	37.35
1992	44.65	0.16	37.51
1993	45.10	0.16	37.77
1994	44.34	0.16	37.24
1995	43.83	0.16	36.82
1996	43.38	0.16	36.44
1997	41.59	0.16	34.94

Note: 1.   EMP is the average number of employees in SOIEs with independent accounting systems. It is calculated as the arithmetic average of consecutive year-end figures. Jefferson et al., 1996, p. 173 source these data directly from China's State Statistical Bureau for the years 1980–92. The fundamental integrity of these data is assumed although there appears to be some minor anomalies (see Jefferson et al., 1992, p. 241). Most Chinese statistical publications do not provide separate figures for employees in SOIEs with independent accounting systems. Given that those with independent accounting systems produce the vast majority of output, any difference is likely to be minor. For example, the Jefferson et al., 1992, p. 173 data series states that in 1992 the average number of employees in SOIEs with independent accounting systems is 44.65. SSB, 1996, p. 402 states that the average number of employees in all SOIEs is 44.97. The data from 1992*–97 is the number of employees in all SOIEs and comes from SSB, 1994–1998. In calculating TFP it is therefore assumed that the growth rate in employment in total SOIEs is equal to the growth rate in employment for SOIEs with independent accounting systems. Given the extremely small number of employees in SOIEs without independent accounting systems, this assumption is reasonable. EXC is the percentage of employees excluded on the basis that they are not involved in industrial production. Jefferson et al., 1996, p. 171 estimate that in 1992 this percentage was equal to 16 percent. On the basis of several sample surveys they showed that this percentage has remained almost constant since 1980. It is therefore assumed that this constancy continues until 1997. LAB is the average number of employees in SOIEs involved in industrial production. It is calculated by simply deducting the number of workers implied by the percentage expressed in (EXC) from (EMP).

Table A6   Investment productivity modeling data

	GDP	SBA	DL	FI	SRF
1981	5.2	5.55	2.51	0.75	10.96
1982	9.1	5.27	3.33	1.14	13.49
1983	10.9	5.72	2.96	1.12	14.29
1984	15.2	5.87	3.60	0.99	15.10
1985	13.5	4.55	5.69	1.02	17.11
1986	8.8	4.47	6.45	1.35	18.32
1987	11.6	4.15	7.29	1.52	18.73
1988	11.3	2.89	6.55	1.84	19.89
1989	4.1	2.16	4.51	1.72	17.68
1990	3.8	2.12	4.77	1.53	15.93
1991	9.2	1.76	6.08	1.48	16.56
1992	14.2	1.30	8.31	1.76	18.96
1993	13.5	1.40	8.87	2.76	24.72
1994	12.6	1.13	8.55	3.78	24.66
1995	10.5	1.06	7.18	3.93	22.93
1996	9.6	0.92	6.74	4.05	22.70
1997	8.8	0.94	6.42	3.60	22.96
1998	7.8	1.53	7.07	3.34	24.71
1999	7.1	2.26	6.98	2.45	24.58
2000	8.0	2.36	7.52	1.90	25.25

Note: GDP is the growth rate of real GDP (%). The data is from SSB, 2001, p. 41. SBA is fixed investment funded through state budget appropriations as a percentage of GDP. The data are from SSB, 2001, p. 159. DL is fixed investment funded through domestic bank loans as a percentage of GDP. The source is the same as SBA. FI is fixed investment funded through foreign investment as a percentage of GDP. The source is the same as SBA. SRF is fixed investment funded through self-raised funds as a percentage of GDP. The source is the same as SBA.

References

ACFB (*Almanac of China's Finance and Banking*) (various years), English (EE) and Chinese (CE) editions, Beijing: People's China Publishing House.

ACFERT (*Almanac of China's Foreign Economics Relations and Trade*) (various years), Hong Kong: China Resources Advertising Company.

Aoki, M. (1995), 'Controlling Insider Control: Issues in Corporate Governance in Transition Economies', in M. Aoki and H. Kim (eds), *Corporate Governance in Transitional Economies: Insider Control and the Role of Banks*, Washington, DC: World Bank, pp. 3–30.

Arestis, P. and P. Demetriades (1997), 'Financial Development and Economic Growth: Assessing the Evidence', *Economic Journal*, 107, 783–799.

Atje, R. and B. Jovanovic (1993), 'Stock Markets and Development', *European Economic Review*, 37 (2/3), 632–640.

Banerjee, A., J. Dolado, J. Galbraith and D. Hendry (1993), *Cointegration, Error Correction, and the Econometric Analysis of Non-Stationary Data*, Oxford: Oxford University Press.

Banerjee, A., T. Besley and T. Guinnane (1994), 'The Neighbour's Keeper: the Design of a Credit Cooperative with Theory and a Test', *Quarterly Journal of Economics*, 109, 491–515.

BIS (Bank of International Settlements), *Consolidated International Banking Statistics*. Available at http://www.bis.org

Bencivenga, V. and B. Smith (1991), 'Financial Intermediation and Endogenous Growth', *Review of Economic Studies*, 58, 195–209.

Bhatt, V. (1982), 'On a Development Bank's Selection Criteria for Industrial Projects', in W. Diamond and V. Raghavan (eds), *Aspects of Development Bank Management*, Baltimore: Johns Hopkins University Press, pp. 60–79.

Bonin, J. and Y. Huang (2001), 'Dealing with the Bad Loans of the Chinese Banks', *Journal of Asian Economics*, 12, 197–214.

Bonser-Neal, C. and K. Dewenter (1999), 'Does Financial Market Development Stimulate Savings? Evidence from emerging stock markets', *Contemporary Economic Policy*, 17 (3). Obtained from an electronic source.

Borish, M., W. Ding and M. Noel (1997), 'A Review of Bank Performance During Transition in Central Europe', *Communist Economies and Economic Transformation*, 9 (3), 337–357.

140 *Financial reform and economic development in China*

Bowles, P. and G. White (1992), 'The Dilemmas of Market Socialism: Capital Market Reform in China – Part II: Shares', *The Journal of Development Studies*, 28 (4), 575–594.

Broadman, H. (1995), *Meeting the Challenges of Chinese Enterprise Reform*, Washington, DC: World Bank.

Byrd, W. (1983), *China's Financial System: the Changing Role of Banks*, Boulder, CO: Westview Press.

Cai, K. (1999), 'Outward Foreign Direct Investment: a Novel Dimension of China's Integration into the Regional and Global Economy', *China Quarterly*, 160, 856–880.

Chai, J.C.H. (1981), 'Domestic Money and Banking Reform in China', *Hong Kong Economic Papers*, 14, 37–52.

Chai, J.C.H. (1990), 'Is China Becoming a Leading Pacific Economy?', in D. Cassel and G. Heidck (eds), *China's Contemporary Reforms and Development Strategy*, Nomos: Baden-Baden, pp. 145–163.

Chai, J.C.H. (1994), 'Savings and Investment in China', *Savings and Development*, XVIII (4), 497–516.

Chai, J.C.H. (1998), *China: Transition to a Market Economy*, Oxford: Clarendon Press.

Chai, J.C.H. (2000), 'Introduction', in J.C.H. Chai (ed.), *The Economic Development of Modern China Vol. 1: pre-war economic development*, Cheltenham, UK and Brookfield, US: Edward Elgar, pp. XI-XLII.

Chai, J.C.H. and G. Docwra (1997), 'Reform of Large and Medium State Industrial Enterprises: Corporatization and Restructure of State Ownership', in M. Brosseau, H. Kuan and Y.Y. Kueh (eds), *China Review 1997*, Hong Kong: Chinese University Press, pp. 162–180.

Chandavarkar, A. (1992), 'Of Finance and Development: Neglected and Unsettled Questions', *World Development*, 20 (1), 133–142.

Charemza, W. and D. Deadman (1997), *New Directions in Econometric Practice*, Cheltenham, UK and Brookfield, US: Edward Elgar.

Chen, A. (1994), 'Chinese Industrial Structure in Transition: the Emergence of Stock-offering firm', *Comparative Economic Studies*, 36 (4), 1–19.

Chen, K., G. Rawski, H. Wang and Y. Zheng (1988), 'Productivity Change in Chinese Industry, 1953–1985', *Journal of Comparative Economics*, 12 (4), 570–591.

Cheng, H., H. Fong and T. Mayer (1997), 'China's Financial Reform and Monetary Policy: issues and strategies', in Joint Economic Committee, Congress of the United States, *China's Economic Future*, New York: M.E. Sharpe, pp. 203–220.

CMS (*China Monthly Statistics*) (various issues), Beijing: China Statistical Information and Consultancy Services Center.

Cho, Y. (1986) 'Inefficiencies from Financial Liberalization in the Absence of

Well-Functioning Equity Markets', *Journal of Money, Credit and Banking*, 18 (2), 191–200.

Chou, W. and Y. Shih (1998), 'The Equilibrium Exchange Rate of the Chinese Renminbi', *Journal of Comparative Economics*, 26 (1), 165–174.

Chow, G. (1986), 'Chinese Statistics', *American Statistician*, XL, 191–196.

Corbett, J. (1994), 'An Overview of the Japanese Financial System', in N. Dimsdale and M. Prevezer (eds), *Capital Markets and Corporate Governance*, Oxford: Clarendon Press, pp. 306–324.

Corsetti, G., P. Pesenti and N. Roubini (1999), 'Paper Tigers? A Model of the Asian Crisis', *European Economic Review*, 43 (7), 1211–1236.

Courakis, A. (1984), 'Constraints on Bank Choices and Financial Repression in Less Developed Countries', *Oxford Bulletin of Economics and Statistics*, 46 (4), 341–370.

Cull, R. and C. Xu (2000), 'Bureaucrats, State Banks, and the Efficiency of Credit Allocation: The Experience of Chinese State-Owned Enterprises', *Journal of Comparative Economics*, 28 (1), 1–31.

Davidson, R., D. Hendry, F. Srba and S. Yeo (1978), 'Econometric Modelling of the Aggregate Time-Series Relationship between Consumer's Expenditure and Income in the United Kingdom', *Economic Journal*, 88, 661–692.

Demetriades, P. and K. Luintel (1996a), 'Banking Sector Policies and Financial Development in Nepal', *Oxford Bulletin of Economics and Statistics*, 58 (2), 355–372.

Demetriades, P. and K. Luintel (1996b), 'Financial Development, Economic Growth and Banking Sector Controls: evidence from India', *Economic Journal*, 106, 359–374.

Demetriades, P. and K. Luintel (1997), 'The Direct Costs of Financial Repression: Evidence from India', *Review of Economics and Statistics*, 79 (2), 311–320.

Demirguc-Kunt, A. and R. Levine (1996), 'Stock Markets, Corporate Finance and Economic Growth: an overview', *World Bank Economic Review*, 10 (2), 223–239.

Diamond, W. and V. Raghavan (1982), 'Goals and Strategies' in W. Diamond and V. Raghavan (eds) (1982), *Aspects of Development Bank Management*, Baltimore: Johns Hopkins University Press, pp. 33–340.

Diaz-Alejandro, C. (1985), 'Good-bye Financial Repression, Hello Financial Crash', *Journal of Development Economics*, 19 (1–2), 1–24.

Ding, J. (1998), 'China's Foreign Exchange Black Market: Analysis of Exchange Rate Policy', *The Developing Economies*, XXXVI, 24–44.

Dipchand, C., Y. Zhang and M. Ma (1994), *The Chinese Financial System*, Westport, CT: Greenwood Press.

Duntamen, G. (1989), *Principal Components Analysis*, London, Sage.

Eggerstedt, H., R. Brideau-Hall and S. van Wijnbergen (1995), 'Measuring

Capital Flight: a case study of Mexico', *World Development*, 23 (2), 211–232.

Eichengreen, B., M. Mussa, G. Dell'Ariccia, E. Detragiache, G. Milesi-Ferretti and A. Tweddie (1998), *Liberalizing Capital Movements: some analytical issues*, Washington, DC: IMF.

ESMFB (*Emerging Stock Markets Factbook*) (various years), Washington, DC: International Finance Corporation.

Feder, G., L. Lau, Y. Lin and X. Luo (1989), 'Agricultural Credit and Farm Performance in China', *Journal of Comparative Economics*, 13 (4), 508–526.

Feder, G., L. Lau, Y. Lin and X. Luo (1993), 'The Nascent Rural Credit Market in China', in K. Hoff, A. Braverman and J. Stiglitz (eds), *The Economics of Rural Organization: theory, practice and policy*, Washington, DC: World Bank, pp. 109–130.

Fishlow, A. (1986), 'External Borrowing and Debt Management', in R. Dornbusch and L. Helmers (eds), *The Open Economy: tools for policy makers*, New York: Oxford University Press, pp. 187–222.

Fry, M. (1982), 'Models of Financially Repressed Developing Economies', *World Development*, 10 (9), 731–750.

Fry, M. (1995), 'Financial Development in Asia: Some Analytical Issues', *Asian-Pacific Economic Literature*, 9 (1), 40–57.

Fry, M. (1997a), 'In Favour of Financial Liberalisation', *Economic Journal*, 107, 754–770.

Fry, M. (1997b), 'Interest Rate Liberalization and Monetary Control in China', in K. Gupta (ed.), *Experiences with Financial Liberalization*, Boston: Kluwer Academic Publishers, pp. 69–100.

Gelb, A. (1989), *Financial Policies, Growth and Efficiency*, Policy Planning and Research Working Paper 202, Washington, DC: World Bank.

Gemmell, N. (1988), 'Debt and the Developing Countries: A Simple Model of Optimal Borrowing', *Journal of Development Studies*, 24 (2), 197–213.

Ghate, P. (1992), 'The Interaction Between the Formal and Informal Financial Sectors: the Asian Experience', *World Development*, 20 (6), 859–872.

Gillis, M., D. Perkins, M. Roemer and D. Snodgrass (1996), *Economics of Development*, New York: W.W. Norton & Company.

Girardin, E. (1997), *Banking Sector Reform and Credit Control in China*, Paris: OECD Development Centre.

Girardin, E. and S. Bazen (1998), 'An Empirical Study of Urban Credit Cooperatives in China', *International Review of Applied Economics*, 12 (1), 141–155.

Girardin, E. and P. Xie (1997), *Urban Credit Cooperation in China*, OECD Technical Paper No. 125, Paris: OECD Development Centre. Available at: www.oecd.org

Goldsmith, R. (1969), *Financial Structure and Development*, New Haven, CT: Yale University Press.

Gorton, G. and A. Winton (1998), 'Banking in Transitional Economies: Does Efficiency Require Instability', *Journal of Money, Credit and Banking*, 30 (3). Obtained from an electronic source.

Greenwood, J. and B. Jovanovic (1990), 'Financial Development, Growth, and the Distribution of Income', *Journal of Political Economy*, 98 (5), 1076–1107.

Gregory, N. and S. Tenev (2001), 'The Financing of Private Enterprise in China', *Finance and Development*, 38 (1). Available on-line at: http://www.imf.org/external/pubs/ft/fandd/2001/03/gregory.htm

Griffith-Jones, S. (1995), 'Introductory Framework', in S. Griffith-Jones and Z. Drabek (eds), *Financial Reform in Central and Eastern Europe*, New York: St. Martin's Press, pp. 3–16.

Griffith-Jones, S. and E. FitzGerald (1995), 'Financial Sector Development in Central and Eastern Europe', in S. Griffith-Jones and Z. Drabek (eds), *Financial Reform in Central and Eastern Europe*, New York: St. Martin's Press, pp. 223–246.

Gunter, F. (1996), 'Capital Flight from the People's Republic of China: 1984–1994', *China Economic Review*, 7 (1), 77–96.

Gurley, J. and E. Shaw (1955), 'Financial Aspects of Economic Development', *American Economic Review*, 45 (4), 515–538.

Harris, R. (1997), 'Stock Markets and Development: a Reassessment', *European Economic Review*, 41 (1), 139–146.

He, D. (1994), 'The Stock Market and Industrial Performance: Lessons from the West for Stock Market Development in China', in Q. Fan and P. Nolan (eds), *China's Economic Reforms: the Costs and Benefits of Incrementalism*, New York: St. Martin's Press, pp. 191–217.

Hellman, T., K. Murdock and J. Stiglitz (1997), 'Financial Restraint: Toward a New Paradigm', in M. Aoki, H. Kim and M. Okuno-Fujiwara (eds), *The Role of Government in East Asian Economic Development*, Oxford: Clarendon Press, pp. 163–207.

Hermes, N. and R. Lensink (2000), 'Financial System Development in Transition Economies', *Journal of Banking and Finance*, 24 (4), 507–524.

Heytens, P. and C. Karacadag (2001), *An Attempt to Profile the Finances of China's Enterprise Sector*, IMF Working Paper No. WP/01/182. Available at: http://www.imf.org/external/pubs/ft/wp/2001/wp01182.pdf

Hu, X. (1996), 'Reducing State Owned Enterprises Social Burdens and Establishing a Social Insurance System', in H. Broadman (ed.), *Policy Options for Reform in China's State Owned Enterprises*, Washington, DC: World Bank, pp. 125–148.

Huang, Y. (1995), 'Issues in the Reform of China's Rural Financial System', in O.K. Tam (ed.), *Financial Reform in China*, London: Routledge, pp. 131–142.

IMF (International Monetary Fund) (1994), *Capital Account Convertibility: review of experience and implications for IMF policies*, Washington, DC: International Monetary Fund.

IMF (International Monetary Fund) (1999), *World Economic Outlook, May 1999*, Washington, DC: International Monetary Fund.

IMF (International Monetary Fund), *Annual Report on Exchange Rate Arrangements and Exchange Rate Restrictions (AREAER)*, Washington, DC: International Monetary Fund.

IMF (International Monetary Fund), *Balance of Payments Statistics Yearbook (BOPS)*, Washington, DC: International Monetary Fund.

IMF (International Monetary Fund), *International Financial Statistics Yearbook (IFS)*, Washington, DC: International Monetary Fund.

Jefferson, G., T. Rawski and Y. Zheng (1992), 'Growth, Efficiency, and Convergence in China's State and Collective Industry', *Economic Development and Cultural Change*, 20 (2), 239–266.

Jefferson, G., T. Rawski and Y. Zheng (1996), 'Chinese Industrial Productivity: Trends, Measurements Issues and Recent Developments', *Journal of Comparative Economics*, 23 (2), 146–180.

Jefferson, G., T. Rawski, L. Wang and Y. Zheng (2000), 'Ownership, Productivity Change and Financial Performance in Chinese Industry', *Journal of Comparative Economics*, 28, 786–813.

Jensen, M. and W. Meckling (1976), 'Theory of the Firm: Managerial Behavior, Agency Costs and Ownership Structure', *Journal of Financial Economics*, 3 (4), 305–360.

Kane, J. (1983), *Development Banking: an economic appraisal*, Lexington, MA: Lexington Books.

Khan, M. and A. Senhadji (2000), *Financial Development and Economic Growth Overview*, IMF Working Paper Wp/00/209.

Kueh, Y.Y. (1992), 'Foreign Investment and Economic Change in China', *China Quarterly*, 131, 637–690.

Kueh, Y.Y. (1999), 'Investment Financing and the Profitability Criterion', in Y.Y. Kueh, J.C.H. Chai and G. Fan (eds), *Industrial Reform and Macroeconomic Instability in China*, Oxford: Oxford University Press, pp. 121–145.

Kumar, A., N. Lardy, W. Albrecht and T. Chuppe (1997), *China's Non-Bank Financial Institutions: Trust and Investment Companies*, Washington, DC: World Bank.

Kwan, A., Y. Wu and J. Zhang (1999), 'Fixed Investment and Economic Growth in China', *Economics of Planning*, 9 (1), 73–84.

Lardy, N. (1995), 'The Role of Foreign Trade and Investment in China's Economic Transformation', *China Quarterly*, 144, 1065–1082.

Lardy, N. (1998a), *China's Unfinished Economic Revolution*, Washington, DC: Brookings Institution Press.

Lardy, N. (1998b), 'China and the Asian Contagion', *Foreign Affairs*, 77 (4), 78–88.

Lardy, N. (1999), *When Will China's Financial System Meet China's Needs?*, paper presented at the Conference on Policy Reform in China, Stanford University, November 18–20, 1999. Available at: http://www.brook.edu/views/papers/lardy/19991118.htm

Lardy, N. (2001), 'China's Worsening Debts', *Financial Times*, 22 June, 2001.

Laurenceson, J. and J.C.H. Chai (1998), 'Financial Liberalization and Financial Depth in China', *Savings and Development*, XXII (4), 393–412.

Laurenceson, J. and J.C.H. Chai (2001), 'State Banks and Economic Development in China', *Journal of International Development*, 13, 211–225.

Lee, Y. (1997), 'Bank Loans, Self Financing, and Grants in China's SOEs: Optimal Policy under Incomplete Information', *Journal of Comparative Economics*, 24 (2), 140–160.

Levine, R. (1997), 'Financial Development and Economic Growth: Views and Agenda', *Journal of Economic Literature*, XXXV (II), 688–726.

Levine, R and S. Zervos (1998), 'Stock Markets, Banks and Economic Growth', *American Economic Review*, 88 (3), 537–558.

Li, K.W. (1994), *Financial Repression and Economic Reform in China*, Westport: Praeger.

Li. K.W and T. Liu (2001), 'Financial Liberalization and Growth in China's Economic Reform', *World Economy*, 24 (5), 673–687.

Liu, S. (1999), 'China's Experience in Small and Medium Financial Institution Resolution', in Bank for International Settlements (ed.), *Strengthening the Banking System in China: issues and experience*, Basel: Bank for International Settlements, pp. 298–303. Available at http://www.bis.org

Liu, T. and K.W. Li (2001), 'Impact of Liberalization of Financial Resources in China's Economic Growth: Evidence from Provinces', *Journal of Asian Economics*, 12, 245–262.

Long, M. and S. Sagari (1991), 'Financial Reform in European Economies in Transition', in P. Marer and S. Zecchini (eds), *The Transition to a Market Economy, Vol. 2*, Paris: OECD, pp. 430–442.

Ma, S. (1995), 'Shareholding System Reform: the Chinese Way of Privatisation', *Communist Economies and Economic Transformation*, 7 (2), 159–174.

Makin, T. (1994), *International Capital Mobility and External Account Determination*, New York: St. Martin's Press.

Manoharan, T. (1992), 'Credit and Financial Institutions at the Rural Level in

China', in E. Vermeer (ed.), *From Peasant to Entrepreneur: growth and change in rural China*, Wageningen: Pudoc, pp. 183–215.

Mayer, C. (1994), 'Stock-markets, Financial Institutions, and Corporate Governance', in N. Dimsdale and M. Prevezer (eds), *Capital Markets and Corporate Governance*, Oxford: Clarendon Press, pp. 179–194.

McDonald, D. (1982), 'Debt Capacity and Developing Country Borrowing: a Survey of Literature', *IMF Staff Papers*, 29, 603–646.

McKibbin, W. and K.K. Tang (2000), 'Trade and Financial Reform in China: Impacts on the World Economy', *World Economy*, 23 (8), 979–1003.

McKinnon, R. (1973), *Money and Capital in Economic Development*, Washington, DC: Brookings Institution.

McKinnon, R. (1991), 'Financial Control in the Transition from Classical Socialism to a Market Economy', *Journal of Economics Perspectives*, 5 (4), 107–122.

McKinnon, R. (1993), *The Order of Economics Liberalization: financial control in the transition to a market economy*, Baltimore, MD: Johns Hopkins University Press.

McKinnon, R. (1994), 'Financial Growth and Macroeconomic Stability in China, 1978–1992: Implications for Russia and Other Transitional Economies', *Journal of Comparative Economics*, 18 (3), 438–469.

McKinnon, R. and H. Pill (1996), 'Credible Liberalizations and International Capital Flows: the "Overborrowing Sydrome"', in T. Ito and A. Krueger (eds), *Financial Deregulation and Integration in East Asia*, Chicago: University of Chicago Press, pp. 7–37.

Mehran, H., M. Quintyn, T. Nordman and B. Laurens (1996), *Monetary and Exchange System Reform in China: an experiment in gradualism*, Washington, DC: IMF.

Mookerjee, R. and Q. Yu (1999), 'An Empirical Analysis of Equity Markets in China', *Review of Financial Economics*, 8 (1). Obtained from an electronic source.

Naughton, B. (1992), 'Implications of State Monopoly over Industry and its Relaxation', *Modern China*, 18 (1), 14–41.

Odedokun, M. (1997), 'Relative Effects of Public Versus Private Investment Spending on Economic Efficiency and Growth in Developing Countries', *Applied Economics*, 29 (10), 1325–1336.

OECD (1995), *Financial Market Trends*, Paris: OECD.

Okuda, H. (1990), 'Financial Factors in Economic Development: a Study of the Financial Liberalization Policy in the Philippines', *Developing Economies*, 28 (3), 240–270.

Park, A. and K. Sehrt (1999), *Tests of Financial Intermediation and Banking Reform in China*, William Davidson Institute Working Paper No. 270. Available at: eres.bus.umich.edu/docs/workpap-dav/wp270.pdf

Park, Y. (1994), 'Concepts and Issues', in H. Patrick and Y. Park (eds), *The Financial Development of Japan, Korea and Taiwan: growth, repression and liberalization*, Oxford: Oxford University Press, pp. 3–26.

Patrick, H. (1994), 'Comparisons, Contrasts, and Implications', in H. Patrick and Y. Park (eds), *The Financial Development of Japan, Korea and Taiwan: growth, repression and liberalization*, Oxford: Oxford University Press, pp. 325–371.

Pei, M. (1998), 'The Political Economy of Banking Reforms in China, 1993–1997', *Journal of Contemporary China*, 7 (18), 321–350.

PBC (People's Bank of China), *China Financial Outlook*, Beijing: China Financial Publishing House.

Pesaran, M. and B. Pesaran (1997), *Working with Microfit 4.0*, Oxford: Oxford University Press.

Pesaran, M. and Y. Shin (1999), 'An Autogressive Distributed Lag Modelling Approach to Cointegration Analysis', in S. Strom, A. Holly and P. Diamond (eds), *Centennial Volume of Ragnar Frisch*, Cambridge: Cambridge University Press. Available at: http://www.econ.cam.ac.uk/faculty/pesaran/ADL.pdf

Popov, V. (1999), 'The Financial System in Russia Compared to other Transitional Economies: the Anglo-American model versus the German-Japanese model', *Comparative Economics Studies*, 4 (1). Obtained from an electronic source.

Rana, P. (1995), 'Reform Strategies in Transitional Economies: Lessons from Asia', *World Development*, 23 (7), 1157–1169.

Ren, R. (1997), *China's Economic Performance in International Perspective*, Paris: OECD.

Roemer, M. (1986), 'Simple Analytics of Segmented Markets', *World Development*, 4 (3), 429–439.

Rowstowsi, J. (1995), 'The Banking System, Credit and the Real Sector in Transition Economies' in J. Rowstowsi (ed.), *Banking Reform in Central Europe and the Former Soviet Union,* Budapest: Central European University Press, pp. 16–41.

Sachs, J. and W.T. Woo (1997), 'China's Economic Growth: explanations and the tasks ahead', in Joint Economic Committee (ed.), Congress of the United States, *China's Economic Future*, New York: M.E. Sharpe, pp. 70–100.

Santeromo, A. (1984), 'Modelling the Banking Firm', *Journal of Money, Credit and Banking*, 16 (4), 576–616.

Scher, M. (2001), *Postal Savings and the Provision of Financial Services: policy issues and Asian experiences in the use of the postal infrastructure for savings mobilization*, Discussion paper of the United Nations Department of Economic and Social Affairs No. 22. Available at: http://www.un.org/esa/esa01dp22.pdf

Scholtens, B. (2000), 'Financial Regulation and Financial System Architecture in Central Europe', *Journal of Banking and Finance*, 24, 525–553.

Schumpter, J. (1912), 'Theorie der Wirtschaftlichen Entwicklung' [The Theory of Economic Development], Leipzig, Dunker & Humblot: translated by R. Opie (1934), Cambridge, MA: Harvard University Press.

Shaw, E. (1973), *Financial Deepening in Economic Development*, New York: Oxford University Press.

Sicular, T. (1998), 'Capital Flight and Foreign Investment: Two tales from China and Russia', *World Economy*, 21 (5), 589–602.

Singh, A. (1990), 'The Stock Market in a Socialist Economy', in P. Nolan and F. Dong (eds), *The Chinese Economy and its Future*, Oxford: Polity Press, pp. 161–178.

Singh, A. (1997), 'Financial Liberalization, Stock Markets and Economic Development', *Economic Journal*, 107, 771–782.

Singh, A. and B. Weiss (1998), 'Emerging Stock Markets, Portfolio Capital Flows and Long-term Economic Growth: Micro and Macroeconomic Perspectives', *World Development*, 26 (4), 607–622.

Song, H., X. Liu and R. Romilly (1998), 'Stock Returns and Volatility: an Empirical Study of Chinese Stock Markets', *International Review of Applied Economics*, 12 (1), 129–139.

Spencer, M. (1995), 'Securities Markets in China', *Finance and Development*, 32 (2), 28–31.

SSB (State Statistical Bureau) (various years), *China Statistical Yearbook* (*CSY*), English (EE) and Chinese (CE) editions, Beijing: China Statistical Publishing House.

SSO (State Statistical Office), 1990, *Zhongguo Shangye Waijing Tongji Ziliao 1955–1988* (*ZGSYWJTJZL 1955–1988*) [China Statistical Data on Commerce and Foreign Economics Relations], Beijing: China Statistical Publisher.

Stiglitz, J. (1990), 'Peer Monitoring and Credit Markets', *World Bank Economic Review*, 4, 351–366.

Stiglitz, J. (1994), 'The Role of the State in Financial Markets', in M. Bruno and B. Pleskovic (eds), *Proceedings of the World Bank Annual Conference on Development Economics 1993*, Supplement to the World Bank Economic Review and the World Bank Research Observer, Washington, DC: World Bank, pp. 19–52.

Stiglitz, J. and M. Uy (1996), 'Financial Markets, Public Policy, and the East Asian Miracle', *World Bank Research Observer*, 11 (2), 249–276.

Su, D. and B. Fleisher (1998), 'Risk, Return and Regulation in Chinese Stock Markets', *Journal of Economics and Business*, 50 (3), 239–256.

Tam, O.K. (1986), 'Reform of China's Banking System', *World Economy*, 9 (4), 427–440.

Tam, O.K. (1988), 'Rural Finance in China', *China Quarterly*, 113, 60–76.

Tam, O.K. (1991), 'Capital Market Development in China', *World Development*, 19 (5), 511–532.

Tam, O.K. (ed.) (1995), *Financial Reform in China*, London: Routledge.

Tam, O.K. (1999), *The Development of Corporate Governance in China*, Cheltenham, UK and Brookfield, US: Edward Elgar Publishing.

Thirlwall, A. (1989), *Growth and Development*, London: Macmillan.

Tsang, S. (1995), 'Informal Credit Markets and Economic Development in Taiwan', *World Development*, 23 (5), 845–855.

Tsang, S. (1997), 'Towards the Full Convertibility of the Renminbi', in M. Brosseau, H. Kuan and Y.Y. Keuh (eds), *China Review 1997*, Hong Kong: Chinese University Press, pp. 235–252.

van Kemenade, W. (1999), 'Besieged: China, Hong Kong, and Taiwan in the Asian Financial Crisis', *Washington Quarterly*, 22 (3), 165–180.

Waters, W. (1997), 'The Link between Total Factor Productivity, Price and Financial Performance, with Illustrations from Air and Rail Transportation', mimeo, Seminar presented at the Department of Economics, University of Queensland.

Watson, A. (1998), 'Conflicts of Interest: Reform of the Rural Credit Cooperatives in China', *MOCT-MOST*, 8, 23–40.

Wei, S. (1996), 'Foreign Direct Investment in China: Sources and Consequences', in T. Ito and A. Krueger (eds), *Financial Deregulation and Integration in East Asia*, Chicago: Chicago University Press, pp. 77–101.

Wong, C., C. Heady and W.T. Woo (1995), *Fiscal Management and Economic Reform in the People's Republic of China*, Hong Kong, Oxford University Press.

Woo, W.T., W. Hai, Y. Jin and F. Fan (1994), 'How Successful has Chinese Economic Reform been? Pitfalls in Opposite Biases and Focus', *Journal of Comparative Economics*, 18 (3), 410–437.

World Bank (1988), *China: Finance and Investment*, Washington, DC: World Bank.

World Bank (1990), *China: Financial Sector Policies and Institutional Development*, Washington, DC: World Bank.

World Bank (1993a), *The East Asian Economic Miracle*, Washington, DC: World Bank.

World Bank (1993b), *The Achievement and Challenge of Price Reform*, Washington, DC: World Bank.

World Bank (1996), *World Development Report 1996: from plan to market*, Washington, DC: World Bank.

World Bank (various years), *Global Development Finance (GDF)*, Washington, DC: World Bank.

Wu, X. (1995), 'China's Financial Institutions', in O.K.Tam (ed.), *Financial Reform in China*, London: Routledge, pp. 83–103.

Wu, Y. (1993), 'Productive Efficiency in Chinese Industry', *Journal of Asian-Pacific Economic Literature*, 7 (2), 58–66.

Xiang, B. (1998), 'The Reform of China's Large State-Owned Enterprises: the Indispensable Role of Stock Markets', in J. Cheng (ed.), *China in the Post-Deng Era*, Hong Kong: Chinese University Press, pp. 311–328.

Xu, X. and Y. Wang (1997), *Ownership Structure, Corporate Governance, and Corporate Performance: The Case of Chinese Stock Companies*, World Bank Working Paper No. 1794. Available at: http://econ.worldbank.org/docs/556.pdf

Xu, X. and Y. Wang (1999), 'Ownership Structure and Corporate Governance in Chinese Stock Enterprises', *China Economic Review*, 10 (1), 75–98.

Yang, H. (1996), *Banking and Financial Control in Reforming Planned Economies*, New York: St. Martin's Press.

Yao, C. (1998), *Stock Market and Futures Market in the People's Republic of China*, Hong Kong: Oxford University Press.

Yi, G. (1994), *Money, Banking and Financial Markets in China*, Boulder, CO: Westview Press.

Yu, Q. (1998), 'Capital Investment, International Trade and Economic Growth in China: evidence in the 1980–90s', *China Economic Review*, 9 (1), 73–84.

Zhang, W. and G. Yi (1997), 'China's Gradual Reform: an historical perspective', in C. Tisdell and J.C.H. Chai (eds), *China's Economic Growth and Transition: Macroeconomic, Regional, Environmental and Other Dimensions*, Brisbane: University of Queensland, pp. 15–39.

Zhongguo Gongye Jingji Ziliao, 1949–1984 [China's Industrial Economic Statistical Data] (1985), Beijing: *Zhongguo Tongji*.

Zhongguo Jinrong [China Finance] (various issues), Beijing: *Zhongguo Jinrong Rongchu Banshe*.

Zhongguo Wujia [China Price] (various issues), Beijing: State Planning Commission.

Zhu, L., Z. Jiang and J. von Braun (1997), *Credit Systems for the Rural Poor in China*, New York: Nova Science Publishers.

Zou, L. and L. Sun (1996), 'Interest Rate Policy and Incentives of State Owned Enterprises in the Transitional China', *Journal of Comparative Economics*, 23 (3), 292–318.

Zuo, X. (2001), 'The Development of Credit Unions in China', paper presented at the conference on Financial Sector Reform in China, Harvard University,

September 11–13, 2001. Available at: http://www.ksg.harvard.edu/cbg/conferences/financial_sector/PostFailuresoftheCreditUnion.pdf

Index